"I have watched his pre: ⎯⎯⎯⎯ ⎯⎯⎯ and respect his insight and understanding. We will always weigh heavily before the Lord any comments or words that Larry Reese feels are from the Father, as we have seen the fruit of his life. He acts like my heavenly Papa."
—*Alice Trammell, Ablaze Ministries*

"I am personally grateful for the heartfelt ministry of Larry B. Reese. I have personally benefited from his mentoring and teaching, as his heartbeat is to instruct us to know God more intimately. Larry has spent close and careful time with the Lord, so the message that comes forth in his writings essentially reveals this. Such a message as being intimate with our heavenly Father is so needed."
—*Jay Powell, Senior Pastor, His Presence Training Center and Church*

"His heart for the Lord and for the greatest good of His people is clearly evident as he ministers the word of God in teaching and in song. He does not just prophesy as all prophets should do, but he also imparts the transforming life of Christ to those who long for it."
—*Gary H. Patterson, Author*

"During a time when men are consumed with all they are doing for the Lord, it is refreshing to encounter a man who is consumed with His presence more than His product. Larry is one such man. From the moment I met Larry, I found him inspiring and contagious in his love and desire for a continuous and deeper relationship with Jesus. As you read the pages of this book you, too, will be engulfed and overwhelmed by that same contagious spirit."
—*Jerry Williams, President of EPIC Ministries, Inc.*

"The need for this ministry is so great, as countless sincere Christians never reach their God given potential-having neither the leader nor the environment to grow. I thank God for this cutting edge ministry."
    —*Steve Sampson, Evangelist & Author*

"Larry has learned his lessons, not in the libraries of men, but in the lap of the Father."
    —*Frank McCarley, Malachi Ministries, International*

"I see in him a delicate balance of the strong voice of a prophet, cradled in a genuine love and compassion for people."
    —*Dustin Pennington, Senior Pastor*
    Cornerstone Fellowship Assembly of God

Being Intimate With God

Larry Reese

AXIOM PRESS

ISBN 1-58169-232-3
For Worldwide Distribution
Printed in the U.S.A.

Axiom Press
P.O. Box 191540 • Mobile, AL 36619
800-367-8203

Table of Contents

Dedication

To my sons and daughters in the faith who have continued in the teachings they have learned over the past years. They are living testimonies of the truths written in this book. To them I dedicate this work for their labor to remain faithful and steadfast in their walk with Jesus Christ.

Introduction

I am very thankful to the Lord for His consistent years of sharing Himself and revealing Himself to me in so many special ways. His love for me as He has revealed it to me has transformed my life. Once one has been so blessed by such a Person as the Lord, you cannot help but mention this kindness and share it with others.

Being Intimate With God is intended to aid people in knowing our heavenly Father better. While many have the desire to know God better but often lack resources, *Being Intimate With God* is such a source—a tool to better acquaint the hungry and searching with God. Its sole purpose is to bring you into a special relationship with a very special Person—the Lord Jesus Christ.

Chapter 1

An Open Door

Relationships take time. They are not always exactly what we expect, and some are harder than others. Since most of us are looking for good ones, there are some things we must first consider: Do we really want a relationship with this person? Are we willing to pay the price for this relationship? Is it worth having a relationship with this person? What am I seeking personally in this relationship? What can I offer this person?

Perhaps questions like these seem a bit strange, especially when we are talking about being intimate with God. Since God knows everything about me, how do I talk about or tell Him about myself, what I am feeling, what I am going through? What is there for me to offer Him in the initial stages of this relationship? God does know us, but we know very little about Him. Because of this, in our earlier stages of getting to know Him, He gives us the opportunity to simply talk while He listens. But we must get some insight into how we approach God—or how He is making Himself available for us to know Him.

In the process of becoming intimate with God, we must allow ourselves to stop thinking of God as unapproachable, but rather we need to see Him as close and reachable. As long as we view our heavenly Father as distant, it will be very difficult for us to know Him.

God's Existence

Now, before we can talk about developing a relationship with God, let us first ask ourselves a basic question: How can we know that there is a God somewhere? What visible proof do we have that God exists? After all, part of our essential makeup is to see and feel things, and to relate to what we see and feel. So if we cannot see or feel God, then how do we respond to God?

> *For that which is known about God is evident to them and made plain in their inner consciousness, because God (Himself) has shown it to them. For ever since the creation of the world His invisible nature and attributes, that is, His eternal power and divinity, have been made intelligible and clearly discernible in and through the things that have been made (His handiworks)* (Romans 1:19-20).

So we can see by this passage of Scripture that God has made Himself evident within us by an inner witness that corresponds with what we see. We see God's creation—the trees, the mountains, the oceans, the world, the stars—and then that which is within us reaches out to want to know more about the God who created it.

Now, if we are reasonable, we will say that in the early stages of developing a relationship with God, despite what we see naturally, we still find it hard to believe that God would want to have anything to do with us. Part of this mindset has to do with what we think about sin—how we feel that God probably does not want to relate to us because we have sinned and we do not feel we can stop sinning.

It is true that we have sinned, but what makes us Christians or those who have the ability to know God up close is what Jesus Christ did for us to allow us to no longer be known as sinners but as God's children.

> *Such hope never disappoints or deludes or shames us, for God's love has been poured out in our hearts through the Holy Spirit Who has been given to us. While we were yet in weakness (powerless to help ourselves), at the fitting time Christ died for (in behalf of) the ungodly. Now it is an extraordinary thing for one to give his life even for an upright man, though perhaps for a noble and lovable and generous benefactor someone might even dare to die. But God shows and clearly proves His (own) love for us by the fact that while we were still sinners, Christ (the Messiah, the Anointed One) died for us (Romans 5:5-8).*

Coming Into His Presence

To simplify things, let us say that we are now those who can approach God and come into His presence, the place where God sits on His throne. Now, we must understand that before any person comes before a king for any reason, he must first prepare himself—clean himself, putting on nice clothes, bettering his overall appearance. But in order to appear before God, we need more than a bath and nice clothes, we need the sacrifice of Jesus Christ to fully cleanse us of sin so that nothing can any longer interfere with our approaching God.

Therefore, since we are now justified (acquitted, made righteous, and brought into right relationship with God) by Christ's blood, how much more (certain is it that) we shall be saved by Him from the indignation and wrath of God. For if while we were enemies we were reconciled to God through the death of His Son, it is much more (certain), now that we are reconciled, that we shall be saved (daily delivered from sin's dominion) through His (resurrection) life (Romans 5:9-10).

We have heard this truth as Christians; however, this must be accepted as truth coming from God concerning our salvation and being restored to Him as His children. It is not good enough to simply know these things in our minds, but the truth of God's Word must find residence deep within our hearts so that we are able to recognize God as He makes Himself more familiar to us in everyday life.

If we do not see ourselves as fully acceptable to God, then it will be very difficult or close to impossible to believe that we can fellowship and even have fun with Him. We must learn that even after we believe the Scriptures about Jesus and His purpose for bringing us salvation, we must continue to live and walk in this truth if we are to become stronger in our faith.

Because if you acknowledge and confess with your lips that Jesus is Lord and in your heart believe (adhere to, trust in, and rely on the truth) that God raised Him from the dead, you will be saved. For with the heart a person believes (adheres to, trusts in, relies on Christ) and so is justified (declared righteous, acceptable to God), and with the mouth he confesses (declares openly and speaks out freely his faith) and confirms (his) salvation (Romans 10:9-10).

We need to understand that God's Word is eternal—it began all things and will end all things. If we accept this truth and go on to understand it, then we will also begin to clearly see that God speaks His word to show Himself to us. He speaks in the form of a Person, and that Person is Jesus Christ. Now, if we have been saved, we have been saved through the Person of Jesus Christ.

Again, we do not want to complicate things. The reason we are saved, the way that we have been saved or made acceptable in God's eyes is through the sacrifice of Jesus Christ, His Son. All of our sins are forgiven. Now, we must accept the fact that as God continues to speak to us through His Word—or through Jesus Christ, we continue to experience salvation daily, as we hear God's voice.

Now we are capable of hearing God each day, but the problem has been we have not responded to Him. In the upcoming chapter, we will talk about how God reveals Himself to us in varying ways, making us better acquainted with Himself outwardly, through what we can identify with through our senses or the things we perceive with our minds that will eventually draw us to Him.

Chapter 2

To Know Him

For God so greatly loved and dearly prized the world that He (even) gave up His only begotten (unique) Son, so that whoever believes in (trust in, clings to, relies on) Him shall not perish (come to destruction, be lost) but have eternal (everlasting) life. For God did not send the Son into the world in order to judge (to reject, to condemn, to pass sentence on) the world, but that the world might find salvation and be made safe and sound through Him (John 3:16-17).

Scripture is very powerful and has the potential to come alive within our hearts when we accept Jesus Christ as our Savior. Now, if we are to walk with God with a clear conscience, then we must trust Him to show us instinctively when things are wrong. Most of the time if we are trying to critique ourselves—judging what is right or what is wrong, we become our worse critics. However, we must grow to know that God always deals with us in love, not out of harsh criticism and judgment. For many of us, it is hard to know God this way. We have often been told that God is a God of judgment and will punish all sin. This is true; however, we must understand that God has judged our personal sin and acquitted us through the blood of Jesus Christ when we accept this sacrifice.

> *He came to that which belonged to Him (to His own—His domain, creation, things, world), and they who were His own did not receive Him and did not welcome Him. But to as many as did receive and welcome Him, He gave the authority (power, privilege, right) to become the children of God, that is, to those who believe in (adhere to, trust in, and rely on) His name. Who owe their birth neither to bloods nor to the will of the flesh (that of physical impulses) nor to the will of man (that of a natural father), but to God (They are born of God!) (John 1:11-13).*

As we walk in this truth, there is a hunger that develops within us. This hunger can also be described as a desire to know God more intimately. If we are sincerely seeking God, then God will reveal Himself to us. We do not discover God; He reveals Himself to us. And once He reveals Himself to us, God intends for us to walk with Him for the rest of our lives as He teaches us His ways.

The whole purpose for Jesus coming to earth was to bring back everything to God that was taken through Satan's deception—but especially the heart and mind of man. God wants our minds restored to Him so that we may understand, know, and comprehend Him as Adam did. In Scripture we read about the beginning relationship that God had with Adam in the Garden. Adam was completely perfect and in love with God in every way, having all of his needs met by God. In addition to this, God expressed Himself to Adam, teaching him about where he was, who he was, and where he came from. This same desire remains in man today.

> *Then the Lord God formed man from the dust of the ground and breathed into his nostrils the breath of spirit of life, and man became a living being* (Genesis 2:7).

When Adam became a living being, it means that he was able to respond to God. He was living and the breath that brought him to life came from God. Everything that has life in it has come from God, since God is the Author of life. It was not until Adam disobeyed God that this life was interrupted. Rather than responding to God inwardly, man began to respond to God outwardly or from outside stimuli—God speaking outwardly, rather than His voice being able to be discerned inwardly. Before Adam dishonored God in the Garden, he was very sensitive to the voice of God speaking to him inwardly. Satan basically robbed man of fellowship with God. Because Adam and Eve disobeyed God, they lost their place in the Garden, but God has restored us to Himself through Jesus Christ.

God Calls Us

If we examine this a bit further we can see that until we accept the ultimate sacrifice of Jesus Christ, we will continue to feel that God is angry with us. He is not. God has been satisfied completely with the sacrifice of His Son. And as we walk in the understanding of this sacrifice, then we can begin to enjoy uninterrupted fellowship with our Father.

God does not condemn or push us away from Himself. He calls and draws us near.

> *And you (He made alive), when you were dead (slain) by (your) trespasses and sins. In which at one time you walked (habitually). You were following the course and fashion of this world (were under the sway of the tendency of this present age), following the prince of the power of the air. (You were obedient to and under the control of) the (demon) spirit that still constantly works in the sons of disobedience (the careless, the rebellious, and the unbelieving, who go against the purposes of God).... But God—so rich is He in His mercy! Because of and in order to satisfy the great and wonderful and intense love with which He loved us, even when we were dead (slain) by (our own) shortcomings and trespasses, He made us alive together in fellowship and in union with Christ; (He gave us the very life of Christ Himself, the same new life with which He quickened Him, for) it is by grace (His favor and mercy which you did not deserve) that you are saved (delivered from judgment and made partakers of Christ's salvation).* (Ephesians 2:1-2, 4-5).

I believe the Lord mentions His love for us many times in Scripture because Satan continues to try and deceive us into believing that God does not love us. However, as we continue to grow in the knowledge of Who God is and who we are in Him, Satan's ability to deceive us diminishes, because we have experience with God. And anyone who experiences God knows that God loves them.

Experience is a great teacher, but experience far exceeds the actual event when we allow what God has revealed to us to change our lives. Earlier we talked about how God makes Himself known to us in what is seen or apparent to our senses. We cannot separate the spiritual from the natural, as God had regular fellowship with Adam each day in the Garden. By this, we know that God participated with that which He had created.

We know through Scripture that God went for long periods of time not speaking to men, and this had to do with the sinful state of man; however, we must know today that God has perfectly drawn us to Himself through Jesus Christ, His Son.

Responding to God

Let's think about how we came to know Jesus Christ. We all have a testimony of some kind. Many people often limit their testimony to what happened at the altar at a church; however, if we are honest, we must say that although we just did not know or recognize it, Christ began to work in our lives much earlier.

Many times people respond or call out to God when difficulties beyond their control happen to them. Since they feel incapable of dealing with the problem at hand, they cry out to God. It is during those times that God hears us because of the sincerity of our cry. We are calling out to Him, but how is He to answer? What are we looking for in His response when we cry out to God? Most of us do not know. But as we begin to recognize God even if it is only crying out to Him in our need, we begin to see that He hears and listens, and we do see some change. Although the changes may not be immediate, we eventually do see them. In my own walk with God I have found that the more I recognize God in the way that He reveals Himself to me, the more I can praise Him for what He does. And the more I praise the Lord, the more it seems He reveals Himself. But there must be a beginning place, where God actually does something that amazes us or that let's us know only God could have done what we have experienced.

> *Now Moses kept the flock of Jethro his father-in-law, the priest of Midian; and he led the flock to the back or west side of the wilderness and came to Horeb or Sinai, the mountain of God. The Angel of the Lord appeared to him in a flame of fire out of the midst of a bush; and he looked, and behold, the bush burned with fire, yet was not consumed. And Moses said, I will now turn aside and see this great sight, why the bush is not burned. And when the Lord saw that he turned aside to see, God called to him out of the midst of the bush and said, Moses, Moses! And he said, Here am I (Exodus 3:1-4).*

Here is a very powerful example of God revealing Himself to one of the most powerful men of the Bible. But we also see that Moses was a common man or shepherd, who was doing his every day job. God reveals Himself and deals with us where we are in life. We know from the history of Moses that he had murdered an Egyptian and had fled from Pharaoh decades earlier, but God had plans for Moses to return to Egypt as the deliverer for the Israelites. But in order for this to happen, God had to introduce Himself to Moses first and make known His will to Moses in a way that he would understand.

Now, we can see what got Moses' attention—a bush that did not burn up. Admittedly, anyone seeing such a sight would be drawn to it. It was meant by God to attract Moses. Once it did and Moses began to approach the bush, God was able to speak to Moses, calling Him by name. We know that Moses had compassion for the Israelites before leaving Egypt, and we can believe that this compassion would be a means by which God would lead Him back as a deliverer. Let's look at the conversation.

> *Also He said, I am the God of your father, the God of Abraham, the God of Isaac, and the God of Jacob. And Moses hid his face, for he was afraid to look at God. And the Lord said, I have surely seen the affliction of My people who are in Egypt, and have heard their cry because of their taskmasters and oppressors; for I know their sorrows and sufferings and trials (Exodus 3:6-7).*

Here we see that God tells Moses what He has seen concerning the Israelites. This is something that Moses also knows and has witnessed with His own eyes. Although Moses may not be acquainted with God as Abraham, Isaac, or Jacob were, he does know the truth about what he has seen in Egypt—the mistreatment of the Jews. So God spoke to him of something that Moses knew and understood. God performed the miraculous by causing the bush to burn without burning up, and then He mentioned the oppression of the Israelites, which Moses was aware of in the natural. God did further things to convince Moses that He is God. In the same way, God will first reveal Himself to us in ways that we can see, like with the burning bush, but then He proves that He is Himself by doing other things that we are not capable of doing.

We should desire to know God as He reveals Himself,

rather than needing miracles on an everyday basis. The miracles serve their purpose, however. Here it was to get Moses attention.

Granted, we may never see God in such a way as He revealed Himself to Moses. But if we will call out to God in desperation, then He will show Himself. But be prepared for God to take you on a journey with Him as He reveals Himself as God, just as He did with Moses.

> Come now therefore, and I will send you to Pharaoh, that you may bring forth My people, the Israelites, out of Egypt (Exodus 3:10).

We know that Moses did exactly what God said he would do. God works in the same way in our lives today.

Chapter 3

Come Closer

We have talked about how many times we do not come to the Lord until there is a problem. Not every situation we run into requires our calling out to the Lord for help, but sometimes problems overwhelm us and we do not have the emotional resources that pull us through. I am not saying that these are the only times that we should call out to God, but I believe that in whatever area God saves us from the most it causes us to love Him most in those areas. But we must understand that God is looking to reveal Himself to us not only in what we see outwardly but to bring us to a point where we can have intimacy with Him.

Before going any further I want to share how to become a part of God's family. We choose to; however, we cannot make the choice of becoming a member of God's family unless He reveals to us how this is done.

Because if you acknowledge and confess with your lips that Jesus is Lord and in your heart believe (adhere to, trust in, and rely on the truth) that God raised Him from the dead, you will be saved. For with the heart a person believes (adheres to, trusts

14

*in, and relies on Christ) and so is justified (de-
clared righteous, acceptable to God), and with the
mouth he confesses (declares openly and speaks out
freely his faith) and confirms (his) salvation*
(Romans 10:9-10).

We equate being saved or the privilege and honor of
being born again with eternal life. There is nothing wrong
with this as it is true, but it goes a bit deeper than simply
living forever. Jesus said that He came that we might have
life and have it more abundantly. The point here is that
Jesus did not want us simply to enjoy natural life alone, but
a vibrant life (abundant life) with our heavenly Father. This
kind of life comes from knowing God intimately, as it is defined:

*And this is eternal life: (it means) to know (to per-
ceive, recognize, become acquainted with, and understand) You, the only true and real God, and
(likewise) to know Him, Jesus (as the) Christ (the
Anointed One, the Messiah), Whom You have sent*
(John 17:3).

Jesus' life was an example of this knowledge and intimacy with our heavenly Father, and that was what He afforded us through not only His death, burial, and
resurrection, but also His life.

Some years ago some people hurt me very deeply, so
deeply that I found myself unwilling to forgive them. I had
never in my entire life hated a group of people more than
these. Rather than go into all the details about what I feel
they did to me, I want to share the results of what happened
to me because I would not forgive them.

I remember I became very sad, had very little energy, and began to feel a deep pain in the center of my heart—my heart was broken since I felt betrayed by those whom I was once very close. Because I would not allow myself to forgive them, the feelings of sadness and the lack of energy kept getting worse.

This had been going on for quite sometime, and I began crying out to the Lord during the day. I was tired—very tired and had little desire to do anything. My friends had hurt me and I tried to punish them by not getting in touch with them. It is very possible that they never really knew how badly they had hurt me.

My Encounter

One particular day I got down on my knees and I began to pray. Oh, I had heard about God. I had even prayed a few times and did things that I thought were pleasing to God—like being kind, going to church, giving a little, etc., but I never found any real and sustaining gladness in doing these things. But as I began to call out to the Lord, I felt the pain more deeply. I know that I was being sincere with God because I was opening my heart, and I had not talked to anyone about what I was feeling. During this time I really felt that I heard Him or something that I thought might be God, but I wasn't sure. A peaceable feeling kept trying to nudge me in a certain direction, which I thought was God.

I can compare what I was feeling was God to what Moses saw in the burning bush. I felt impressed to do a certain thing—to leave home for a while and simply get some rest. I felt that some time away would be good, and this was a week of vacation for me with my employer. I had time to go away, and as I prayed for help, I believed that God was leading me away to clear my head. Or at least, that was what I thought I was doing.

When I did decide to leave, I told my Mom:

"I'm going away for a while," I told her, even feeling a need to tell her that God was telling me to go away. My conviction in leaving was strong, but I had no particular place that I felt drawn to go. All I knew was that I was going somewhere and when I got there, I would know.

When I left home that day I found myself driving northward on the Interstate Highway, still with no particular stopping place in mind. After I'd driven close to two hours, maybe less, I saw a Holiday Inn sign and decided to stay there for the evening. Ironically, during the drive and going away I had felt a lot better. I wasn't as tired, and I felt as though my leaving home was in some form obeying God. I do not remember hearing an audible voice telling me to leave home, but I sensed that it was the right thing to do. And each time I moved forward on what I sensed, I felt better.

I got a room in the Holiday Inn and finally thought I would get some rest when I got inside; however, it seemed that my restlessness grew worse. In addition to this restlessness, I was developing a skin rash and my ears were getting infected. There was no rational explanation for these physical problems, as far as I could tell. But I knew that either something good had to happen or something worse would.

"Lord help me," I found myself saying. "Please help me." These were the most sincere times I believe I had cried out to the Lord. And as I lay on the bed I saw what I will call a very soft light settle into the room. I did not see a person, but it was very apparent that there was a presence in the room. I remember it as being very peaceful, so much so that I almost fell asleep. I felt very comforted by this presence.

"Lord, please help me," I said. "I really need help." Even now I cannot fully understand why I was calling out so, but I honestly felt that I could get help from this presence, and then I heard a voice.

"Larry," I heard.

"Is this the Lord?" I asked, desperately needing to know, and believing that if it were that He would help me. I somehow knew that He would. His presence suggested it.

"I am the Lord," was the answer.

"Lord," I began to open up to Him. "I feel terrible. Something is happening to me, and I do not know why." It began to become clear to me that my hatred from feeling completely and totally let down, my tiredness, and my anger was coming from my unforgiveness toward my friends. This was becoming very clear, and even though I knew it on the drive to the hotel, I did not want to think about it because it was too painful.

"I want you to forgive your friends," He said to me.

"No," I retorted, and remember sitting up with my back against the head board of the bed. I could only think about how they had harmed me and the bitterness within my heart would not allow me to simply let them go. I would not let them go. They needed to be punished for what they had done to me.

"Forgive them," I heard Him say gently, once again.

"I can't," I said. This time my answer was not as abrupt. I was feeling something within giving me the ability or the strength to forgive, but the hurt was just as real as what I was feeling about letting them go. Then the Lord instructed me to do something that I found very interesting. He told me to get the Gideon's Bible out of the side table drawer and go to chapter 6 of the book of Matthew. I want to explain that at that time in my life I was not an avid Bible reader, nor did I know much about the Scriptures, but I did know that what I was hearing was very real. And each time He spoke to me my head cleared, my heart felt better, and I could hear Him, somehow, from within.

And forgive us our debts, as we also have forgiven (left, remitted, and let go of the debts, and have given up resentment against) our debtors. And lead (bring) us not into temptation, but deliver us from the evil one. For Yours is the kingdom and the power and the glory forever, Amen. For if you forgive people their trespasses (their reckless and willful sins, leaving them, letting them go, and giving up resentment), your heavenly Father will also forgive you. But if you do not forgive others their trespasses (their reckless and willful sins, leaving them, letting them go, and giving up resentment), neither will your Father forgive you your trespasses (Matthew 6:12-15).

Once I read this passage of Scripture, it became very clear that I was sick because I would not forgive my friends. I sincerely hated them. But as I read the Scripture here, I began to cry, because not only was I reading it, but it seemed as if the Lord was speaking it to my heart as I read it. This made the experience all the more real—I could not only hear a voice, but I felt the words actually speaking to my heart. I knew that I was opening up to Him because I had been very unwilling to feel anything before. Now I was in a place of decision, I knew that I was a Christian. I had believed in Jesus earlier in life, and it just seemed now that He was more real than ever before.

"Forgive me," I said, really feeling sorry for how I had hated my friends.

"Forgive them," He said to me, His voice very gentle, leading me to simply letting them go. I did not feel guilty, sinful or condemned, I felt that the Lord was reasoning with me to do the right thing, and by doing the right thing, whatever was making me sick would go away.

"I cannot," I told Him.

"Neither can I forgive you," He said, the tone not changing. But it was deep truth. Hearing that He could not forgive me opened my eyes to a very real and clear reality. Then I felt as if His Presence which I had felt so strongly in the room was lifting.

"Please don't leave me," I cried out to Him, reaching for what I could not see, but desperately felt.

"I am not going to leave you," He said softly, then saying again, "Forgive them."

It would not do justice to write what I am writing without being absolutely sure that you understand how much I felt the love of Christ during this time. I felt an overwhelming sense of love and support to do what He was asking. I could not have forgiven them on my own. I did not even want to. I never felt threatened or the possibility of the Lord leaving me in my refusing to forgive them. We must understand that sometimes our feelings are so real to us that we are consumed by them. I did not feel that I was sinning by not forgiving my friends, but I did feel that sin was killing me in this case through my not being willing to forgive them.

"Forgive them," He softly said again, His support all the more evident. Then finally, my heart released them and I gasped.

"I forgive them," I said, and it seemed as if I breathed my last breath.

"I forgive you," He responded gently.

It was after He responded that something even more miraculous happened. My ears opened. I could feel that the infection was gone. He spoke once more to me, saying: "Look in the mirror." I was reluctant because my skin was beginning to turn dark and ugly. I did not like what I had seen recently in the mirror, but I obeyed Him. When I looked, I saw that the rash was completely clear. There was no trace of any rash at all, and my eyes sparkled. The tiredness was gone. The hurting and hatred were gone. I was free from my oppression, and I knew that God had done this.

God had made Himself clear to me in an area where I needed help. Had it not been for Him, I am not sure what I would have done. The way that He treated me through this ordeal, I will never forget—it caused me to love Him in a way that I did not before, plus it caused me to love those who had harmed me so desperately. This within itself was a sovereign move of God. Later, I went to each of them. Ironically, I found them all together in one place—there I asked them to forgive me for the hatred that I'd held against them, apologizing to each of them and further completing the process of releasing and letting them go. They never knew that I had hated them so; however, they did apologize to me for what had happened that caused me to hate them so.

I've shared this testimony and will share others as they are intended to help us better understand and know God in the world through what we actually experience. We all go through hurt, and it is good to know that God intimately carries us through them, if we allow Him to do so.

Chapter 4

He First Loved Us

In this is love; not that we loved God, but that He loved us and sent His Son to be the propitiation (the atoning sacrifice) for our sins (1 John 4:10).

For God did not send the Son into the world in order to judge (to reject, to condemn, to pass sentence on) the world, but that the world might find salvation and be made safe and sound through Him (John 3:17).

For God so greatly loved and dearly prized the world that He (even) gave up His only begotten (unique) Son, so that whoever believes in (trusts in, clings to, relies on) Him shall not perish (come to destruction, be lost) but have eternal (everlasting) life (John 3:16).

Salvation defined means: "Deliverance from the power and effects of sin; liberation from ignorance or illusion; preservation from destruction or failure; deliverance from danger or difficulty" (*The Merriam-Webster Online Dictionary*).

We often hear the word "love" much in Christian circles. We must remember that love is something we do—an act that we perform. This act of love should always come as a natural response to those who are experiencing salvation. I use the word "experiencing" rather than "experienced" because salvation is something we continue to experience. It is an ongoing journey of life and love.

Above I have shared some Scripture verses that most of us are familiar with. Remembering that Jesus is a Person and having a beginning understanding that the Word of God, being Jesus, was made into a human being like us, we can know Him as He appears in Scripture. Now if it is true that the Word of God became a human being, then we must also say that the Word of God, that which is written in the Bible, is seen in the Person of the Lord Jesus Christ. Many of us have often been told things about people—not having met them ourselves, so our opinion is normally based upon what we have heard or thought ourselves. So as Jesus made Himself known to the people, according to what we see in John 1, the people must have been able to see His true affection.

Putting Truth Into Action

For a moment, let me go back to my encounter with the Lord in my hotel room. I had never heard the voice of God before so clearly. I met Him. Literally, I met Him. And because of what He did as I responded to Him, I felt His love for me. Let me explain. I knew that I was sick when I was in that hotel room. In fact, I could tell that I was getting worse as I thought about my friends' betrayal. So I could tell that when the Lord began to speak to me about what was wrong and what the source of my sickness was, I began to feel better. We often feel better when we know the truth—

gaining a better understanding of what our problems are and then being able to solve them; however, true deliverance from any problem must come from not only accepting the truth, but putting it into action.

I knew that I hated my friends. I knew that I was sick because I would not forgive them. I also came to know that I would get worse if I did not forgive them. This understanding came from a Person, whose name is Jesus Christ. Although I did not see Him in the room, He led me to the passage of Scripture that told me what was happening. I was sick because I would not forgive.

Love is something you do. We experience God's love in various ways. I experienced it when He told me the truth about my condition and then healed me. I felt so much better once this healing occurred that I was willing to tell everyone. But mostly, I wanted to forgive those who had harmed me. You see, because of the kindness of the Lord on my behalf, I saw His love for me altogether personally. This is what makes our Savior personable. He cares about us deeply and intimately. Jesus is an intimate Savior because He gets involved with our lives. Salvation is an ongoing experience. We do not allow the Lord to simply get us out of situations and then leave Him alone. If we do this, then we do not continue to see how He is at work in our lives. We cannot simply pray when we lose control of our lives or when situations that overwhelm us come into our lives. Christ is a part of our lives, but only as we allow Him to be.

After I had forgiven my friends, I felt no ill emotion toward them whatsoever. In fact, I could go around them and even desire the very best for them. Before I forgave them, this was not possible. Further, let me say that I had never felt such hatred in my life. Had I continued to live that way, it would have eventually destroyed me. I was already to the point of physical exhaustion, not even wanting to get out of bed in the morning, and it was all because of my not knowing the forgiving power of Jesus Christ.

Our Response to Revelation

Let us ask ourselves a question: When God reveals Himself to us in varying ways, what should be our response? With my experience with the Lord in such a way, it caused me to want to follow Him, to know more about Him, to see Him more clearly. He had healed me completely, and I felt better than I ever had felt in my life. So I wanted to pursue Him.

> *Then you will seek Me, inquire for, and require Me (as a vital necessity) and find Me when you search for Me with all your heart* (Jeremiah 29:13).

We do not altogether know the ways of God, but we see here that God is willing to reveal or share Himself with those who sincerely look for Him. If we pursue Him, then He will reveal Himself to us. Men were created to worship God, and whether they worship God or not, they will worship something. God reveals Himself to us, but it is our responsibility to seek Him out for ongoing intimacy and relationship. Although I was completely satisfied in what Christ did for me in my hotel room, it was not to be the end of my relationship with Him. The Lord desires a consistent and growing fellowship with us. But we cannot be intimate with Him or understand that He wants to be intimate with us unless He shows Himself to us in ways we understand. Salvation is a personal experience that comes from a personal God.

Using Our Faith

Some time later after the event in my hotel, I could not seem to spend enough time with the Lord. I wanted to be with Him all the time. I wanted to hear Him speak to me just like He did in the hotel room. Without being able to hear Him speak so clearly, at times I felt insecure. I needed to know that the Lord was with me like this all the time. This is where faith comes in—active, living faith.

I realize that if God speaks to us so clearly and definitely, then we want to hear Him speak this way all the time. But God wants us to use our faith. He wants us to understand that He is with us all the time and revealing Himself in varying ways that correspond with what we go through as human beings.

So my search continued. My desire grew. I felt compelled to know Him more deeply. Now this desire grew from within me and was based upon what He did for me. When I accepted Jesus as my personal Savior, I believed that I loved Him. But the experience in the hotel gave me a better understanding of what sin does to us, and how Jesus delivered us from it. I experienced the love and delivering power in a way that I could understand more clearly. Sometimes when we say all have sinned, we tend to generalize this into everything I have done up until now has been sin. This is not necessarily true. We sin because we are not hooked up to God or because we do not understand what has happened to us in salvation. If this is not made clear to us, then we will not readily and continually understand the relationship that has been afforded us through Jesus Christ.

As a result of my looking for Christ, I found Him, or rather He revealed Himself to me in a more knowable and tangible way. If we are going to know Christ better, then we must seek Him more deeply. Well, how is it that we seek what cannot be seen? The answer is this: We seek Christ based upon what He has done for us. Experiences are good; however, we must be advised to continue reading God's Word, and spending time with Him silently from time to time so that He can speak to us. Now, these are some of the most powerful times we will ever experience as Christians—when we know God is speaking.

We are told in John 10:4: "When he had brought his own sheep outside, he walks on before them, and the sheep follow him because they know his voice." Then in verse 14, He says: "I am the Good Shepherd; and I know and recognize My own, and My own know and recognize Me."

So we develop a listening ear not by talking so much, but by developing a hearing ear. The Lord speaks to us in what is familiar and what concerns us. Now, again, He may do some dramatic things to get our attention, such as the burning bush, or speaking to me to go to a certain Bible passage, but however He chooses to reveal Himself, we need to allow Him to build upon that revelation. There is not an exact standard of how He will continue to speak to us or reveal Himself to us, but we will recognize Him when He does.

Knowing how God reveals Himself is invaluable. As He reveals Himself we will become more sensitive to His presence. It's like when we know someone so well, we can look at them and tell what they are thinking or feeling. Well, as we grow to know our heavenly Father, we do begin to sense and feel things the way He does. That is how we feel as Christians. We have become a part of His Body. "...We are all parts of one body and members' one of another" (Ephesians 4:25).

With this said I want to share another incident in the next chapter that will further help us understand how God reveals Himself and further leading into how He indwells us.

Chapter 5

Your Mama's God

Earlier we talked about Moses and his experience with God at the burning bush. How this encounter affected his life! We know that Moses could have never been the same once he heard the voice of the eternal God. Neither can we remain the same as the Lord reveals Himself to us—desiring to have a relationship with us that goes beyond going to church twice a week and reading our Bibles first thing in the morning. But we cannot know God this intimately as Moses did, unless we encounter Him.

I have shared one encounter that I had with our Father in the hotel room. This was an incident that changed my life and transformed me. We all have ideas about what God is like, but when we see Him do things that we know only He can do, it causes us to move in a little closer. Just as the Scriptures declare that Moses had to move in a little closer to see why the bush did not burn up, we also want to move in a little closer to see how God did what He did in our personal lives or in the lives of someone close to us. God wants to get our attention—not to wow us, but to reveal Himself to us in ways that we can better know Him. This is how an intimate relationship is begun. God reveals Himself, but it is our responsibility to continue seeking Him once He does. This is a journey that is invaluable, worthy of everyone who has been born again. Christ wants us to know Him.

As we continue moving forward, try to take some time to examine the experiences that I have had with God—those things that go beyond Bible reading, while at the same time, comparing my experiences with what you read in the Bible. When we are familiar with the Scriptures, we will better see how God is related to our experiences. If we can see God working in our experiences and recognize those works as coming from the Bible, then we will better believe and be more qualified to understand the way God does things.

Now, I am not saying that we should go about simply looking for the spectacular or the miraculous. If we are seeking to know God more intimately, He will reveal Himself to us in ways that we will understand. But to get the very best out of the experience, we must be willing to not only seek, but to look forward to the way God shows Himself.

I have mentioned that after my time with the Lord in the hotel room, I wanted to be with Him. Now, I am not talking about going on to heaven. What I felt during that time was what heaven offers: I felt peace, joy, love, safety, and the power of God. In His words to me I felt His authority in a way that I never had. I could tell that God was the ultimate authority, while at the same time, I felt such strong love. That is why I wanted to be with Him.

Basically, I have always been a very happy person; however, there was something in my time with the Lord that caused me to know that something was not completed. Because I could tell by the way the Lord spoke to me that He knew me—that I did not want to forgive or give up my bitterness—and so He encouraged and enabled me to do so. And when I forgave and received this miraculous healing and a deeper sense of His love, I better understood His love.

I do want to make it clear that after the hotel encounter, my desire to know God became more and more powerful. It was as if I were being driven to know Him more. Sometimes, if you have not experienced something for yourself, it is hard to receive an explanation. All I knew was that I wasn't sick any more, and I could not continue hating those who had harmed me. I even took some time to think about it later, realizing that the love that gave me the ability to forgive in such a way was not my own. Not only did the Lord show me that I was wrong and why I was sick, He escorted me through the process of being delivered from what would have eventually destroyed me. I felt that my life was at stake, but God in His love saved me.

Encounters With God

Salvation means that we have deliverance from danger and destruction. I could tell that if I did not get help soon, I knew that something far worse would happen. But how could I have known that forgiving my friends was part of this salvation? The Lord showed me clearly the need to forgive. That is why I began to look for Him. When I say that I was looking for Him, I mean that I tried to go back to the same feelings I had when He spoke to me. Not to be sick again, but to be broken and humble—needing and asking for help. I believed that a disposition such as this would afford me another visit from the Lord; however, now I realize that the Lord wanted *me* and not just *an encounter with me*. I also better understand now that *it was up to Him to show me how to have a relationship rather than continue to seek an encounter.* Encounters are exactly that—they may be a once in a lifetime thing; however, if we are to believe that the Lord wants to be more intimately involved with us, then we must position ourselves, much like I described above—humbly, seeking God in brokenness.

It was a day like any other. I had come home from work, but just could not sit down and relax. I was restless. I had been thinking about the Lord all day, but I could not pray and seek Him like I normally did when I came in after eight hours of work. For some reason this day was different. I had been diligently looking for the Lord—expecting to see Him. Something told me that I would see Him, and I believed what I felt. I do want to point out that I was not obsessed with finding the Lord. As I mentioned earlier, having had such an encounter caused me to desire yet another one—to see the Lord. I believed that since He had been able to speak to me so clearly in the hotel room, I would be able to see more of Him if I knew how to ask Him. How did God want to be seen or known? The desire was developing so I knew that the Lord was drawing me to something deeper, more intimate.

I went to the front room where my aunt was sitting. She and I often talked about the Lord, so that was a very good time of day for me. But today I was having trouble staying awake, and I could not understand why.

"Larry, is the Lord dealing with you?" my aunt asked, seeing that I was having trouble staying awake. All I could do was nod yes, but I wasn't altogether sure whether it was the Lord or not. All I knew was that this strong desire to go to sleep was overtaking me, and since I could not fight it, I decided to go and lay down.

"I'll be back," I told her, then excused myself and went to my bedroom.

A few moments later, I sat on the side of my bed, and it seemed as if the room became dramatically dark. It was not darkness like the absence of light, but thick darkness, though I could still see things moving about in the shadows if I kept my eyes focused. Suddenly I laid down on the bed. I felt as if I began to float and become weightless. I felt afraid as I waited to see what was about to happen. Even though I was in this deep sleep by now or what I thought was sleep, I was very much aware of what was going on around me. I knew everything that was happening—even in the next room where my aunt remained. Somehow, the Lord had enclosed me in a cloud of some kind. I could tell because it looked like a cloud—but more like thick and heavy smoke. At first I was very afraid and my breathing was heavy, but I was soon able to calm myself down. I was afraid because I thought I was going to see something—something of God that could very easily kill me.

This encounter was very different from the hotel experience. I felt a different authority accompanying this, so I was obviously afraid. Nevertheless, I wanted to know what the Lord wanted. Even though I was afraid, I remembered His love from the first encounter and I decided to trust Him now. The darkness seemed to thicken and move in a bit closer as I lay very still on the bed, facing upward. Then He spoke to me.

> *And when you heard the voice out of the midst of the darkness, while the mountain was burning with fire, you came near me, all the heads of your tribes and your elders; And you said, Behold, the Lord our God has shown us His glory and His greatness, and we have heard His voice out of the midst of the fire; we have this day seen that God speaks with man and man still lives* (Deuteronomy 5:23-24).

"I am the Lord, Larry," He spoke to me. "You do not know Me as you should, so I have come to tell you what your mother promised Me before you were born. Do not be afraid," He said.

We must remember that if we are to have an encounter with the Lord—He must introduce and reveal Himself to us. He has a name. He has a purpose. He has a plan for our lives, and He wants us to know this personal plan for ourselves. As we read the Scriptures that I have shared, I want us to put them together with the experience here and what is being said, as we remember that Jesus Christ became a Person—a human being.

And the Word (Christ) became flesh (human, incarnate) and tabernacled (fixed His tent of flesh, lived awhile) among us... (John 1:14).

We should bear this truth in mind as we read about the experiences in this book. Christ became a Person with a voice, the ability to talk to us, share with us, cry with us, work among us, do all that we did, and ultimately die for us. And by the power of God, He was raised again from the dead. So the testimony of the Bible is that our Savior was a human being as well as God. With this in mind, try to picture Jesus speaking to you as a Person, and not as an unreachable God. We already know that our heavenly Father is not angry with us and did not send Jesus to condemn us—so we must now move from knowing this into the next level of His revealing Himself to us personally. Now, if He is to do this, He must also reveal Himself in His deity because He is no longer walking around the world as a human being. So what we will be seeing as we read a little further is how the Lord works with us where we are so that we can understand who He is.

At the sound of His voice, I trembled. I remember my insides shaking. I tried to hide myself, feeling naked, I suppose as Adam did. Somehow I felt completely open to Him as an open book. I remember turning from side to side on the inside, as I got to where I could not move my physical body at all. This frightened me a bit, but as I began to settle down, I knew that He only wanted my attention.

"Do not be afraid," He said once again.

Clouds and darkness are round about Him (as at Sinai); righteousness and justice are the foundation of His throne (Psalm 97:2).

"Before you were born, your mother told Me that if I gave her a son, that she would return him to My service. You are that child. I have come to claim this promise and to make you aware of this. I told your mother that when I made her promise known to you that I would send you to her to let her know that I had made Myself known to you. That time is now."

What was I to do knowing this information? I had never heard this before. Remember, now, Moses had heard about God, but he had never met Him until He encountered Him at the burning bush. But how could I be sure that this was God? It might be assumed that anyone would know that this was God having spoken this way and with the darkness all around me. How could I not know that it was God?

Perhaps I did know, but what must be understood here is that I did not know God this way. I had never heard Him share something about my past, giving me a perception of what would happen in the future. But then He said this:

"I am the God of Abraham, Isaac, and Jacob." I'd read about these men in the Bible, but they were biblical men. I was beginning to believe more that what was happening was really happening, and then He spoke again. "But you do not know Abraham, Isaac, or Jacob. I am the God your Mama talks about." And then I knew Him. Somehow I recognized Him more because I knew God from how my mother talked about Him, but I did not know Him like she did. But I now felt better and knew that I had somehow found Him. Perhaps because I had been called to some kind of ministry was the reason why He was speaking to and revealing Himself to me. At this time, I did not know. But I did know that I wanted to know Him better.

Before I close this chapter and move a bit forward, I want to share that not everyone may experience God in this way. It may not be necessary. However, if we want to know God intimately and personally, then all we need do is seek Him—spending time at His feet. He will reveal Himself.

I will be sharing some other things that will give us a better understanding of how our heavenly Father indwells us and how we can know experientially that He is always with us.

Chapter 6

As Many As Did

But to as many as did receive and welcome Him, He gave the authority (power, privilege, right) to become the children of God, that is, to those who believe in (adhere to, trust in, and rely on) His name (John 1:12).

Here we see that those who welcomed or received Jesus, He gave them the right or ability to become the children of God. And if we continue reading this passage we see that those who become the children of God are those who accept Jesus Christ at His word—believing that He is the Son of God who was sent so that we might be saved from sin.

She will bear a Son, and you shall call His name Jesus (the Greek form of the Hebrew Joshua, which means Savior), for He will save His people from their sins (that is, prevent them from failing and missing the true end and scope of life, which is God) (Matthew 1:21).

As we continue to embrace this truth daily, we begin to

understand how the word of God became a Person. We begin to see that Jesus spoke the Word of God and not so much quoted it. An example would be if we believe God to do something in our lives, we should hold to the truths or promises we find in Scriptures for what we believe God to do. However, if we believe that Jesus Christ—the Word which has always been alive and is God is able to speak as a Person Who came and lived among us, then the promise is made alive within us, and we know that God has given us what we have. If we are to talk to God more intimately, we must grow to know His Word more intimately—not just as that which is written, but that which is spoken also.

> *And this is the confidence (the assurance, the privilege of boldness) which we have in Him; (we are sure) that if we ask anything (make any request) according to His will (in agreement with His own plan), He listens to and hears us. And if (since) we (positively) know that He listens to us in whatever we ask, we also know (with settled and absolute knowledge) that we have (granted us as our present possessions) the requests made of Him* (1 John 14-15).

We understand through teaching from the Scriptures that Jesus told us the Holy Spirit would remind us of the things that Jesus taught. So we must, again, understand that if we know the Scriptures well, the Holy Spirit is able to remind us of the validity of what we believe God for. That is, if it is indeed His will. Being intimate with the Lord requires an acceptance of truth. If we are not willing to let go of what we desire, then we cannot really hear God clearly concerning our desires. I want to talk more about the indwelling

Presence of the Holy Spirit, but before I do, I want to share some things that happened once the Lord told me about the promise He'd made with my mother.

We do know that signs and wonders follow those who believe the truth. But if we are to see those signs and wonders, we must obey the truth. I want to express how important it is that we develop a listening ear to God. You cannot be intimate with someone you cannot hear.

After the Lord revealed to me that I had been given to Him before birth, I thought of it as a good thing; however, as with most Christians, I did not understand the total picture or how these kinds of things work. I could not wait until I was able to talk with my mother about what the Lord had said. When I did, all she could do was cry and nod her head, telling me that I had indeed heard from God. From that moment forward my mother knew that I would possibly be going into some kind of ministry.

God revealed to me His promise between my mother and Himself. Follow the progression of the things here closely. First, the Lord had to get my attention in the hotel room. Then He did some dramatic healing within me, causing me to desire Him more and to learn and know more about Him. That was when I began seeking Him with all of my heart. Then there came another revelation by the Lord. He shared with me what I believe I had wanted to know—or at least part of it. He told me that I belonged to Him. This insight alone gave me the ability to know that I had purpose and that my life was headed somewhere.

We all desire to know that we are going to succeed at something. Father has placed within all of us the desire to succeed and the instinctive knowledge that our lives should have purpose and fulfillment, and we should be satisfied by living in this world. I was beginning to desire to know God more, because He was showing me more about who I am. So signs followed what the Lord had told me that day on the bed. My mother's reactions were confirmation to me that God had indeed spoken. It turns out that she had never told anyone else her promise, not even me.

For I know the thoughts and plans that I have for you, says the Lord, thoughts and plans for welfare and peace and not for evil, to give you hope in your final outcome (Jeremiah 29:11).

Getting to Know God

As these things unfolded before me, I had a sense of being able to see—not that I could see God, but He was acquainting me with His way of doing things. And as I honored Him in what I believed He was requesting of me, I began to understand Him better. This understanding was bringing about a change in my overall attitude. I found that I did not have to stress myself, trying to please God so much. After we accept Jesus Christ as our Savior, there comes a simple and innocent desire to please Him; however, God gently teaches us to serve Him as we know Him. Then as we grow to know Him, He gives us projects to do. I want to carefully point out that these projects are never done without Him— but He works alongside us—aiding us to accomplish what He desires for not only our good, but the good of others also.

I remember once trying so hard to keep the commandments—yes, to keep the commandments. It wasn't so much that I was trying to find an opportunity to keep the commandments of God, but I wanted so desperately to do the right thing. In trying to please God in this manner, I became exasperated. I was a young Christian just trying to please God. Then one day He spoke to me:

"Larry, all I want is for you to love Me. Just love Me." Once He spoke to me, a heavy burden of duty left me. I did love the Lord, but I thought that loving Him meant doing things for Him. Then He spoke to me again: "I do not want you to work for Me, but along with Me. I will give you work to do. Just be patient and love Me. As you love Me, you will begin to better understand who I am and what I desire."

Teacher, which kind of commandment is great and important (the principal kind) in the Law? (Some commandments are light—which are heavy?) And He replied to him, You shall love the Lord your God with all your heart and with all your soul and with all your mind (intellect). This is the great (most important, principal) and first commandment (Matthew 22:36-37).

As we grow to love Christ—being able to see that we have not only been forgiven from what we would consider "general sin," but have been called to be with Him, loving Him, exercising our rights as children with Him, and being able to see and know what He is like experientially. And as we continue to know Him simply by living in the world, we will grow to love Him more as well as others.

Before we go much further I want to begin speaking about the Holy Spirit. I mentioned Him earlier, but I want to talk about Him a bit more as we move forward in our sharing together.

There is much talk about the Holy Spirit, and the opening passage of Scripture that I have used speaks a bit about Him. There is some mystery associated with the indwelling presence of the Holy Spirit, so I want to share with you some things that will better help you know how He indwells us. Once we have talked about this, I believe we will better understand some deeper ways in which the Lord speaks to and reveals Himself to us.

Our heavenly Father deals with us in things that are personal and personable. He wants to be involved in our lives. When we say: "I have a personal relationship with Jesus Christ," we are not saying this because it is what we have heard or have been taught to say, it is because we know who the Holy Spirit is, and He is enabling us to know Jesus Christ better. When we remain open minded and keep an open heart so that the Lord can speak to us as we move forward, the Holy Spirit will be able to give us a deeper understanding of His abiding presence.

Chapter 7

The Holy Spirit

As Christians, we hear a lot about the Holy Spirit but I am not sure we really understand how personable the Holy Spirit is or what He has been called to do. Now we have also heard about the Trinity—the Father, Son, and Holy Spirit. Most of us have a good idea about the Father and the Son, but when it comes to the Holy Spirit, we have questions. I believe that most of the questions come from the mystery often associated with the Holy Spirit and how He works in our lives. Depending on your beliefs or religious background, the Holy Spirit can be associated with a number of things and have varying functions. I would like to share who the Holy Spirit is and has been to me personally, offering a testimony that will better help you know who and what He does. Although much can be said about the Holy Spirit, we will deal with His relationship to Jesus Christ our Savior and what Jesus said about Him during His final days on earth.

Jesus had walked with His disciples for three years. I would imagine that these were some of the most intense times of their lives—teaching, preaching, and traveling during the day, and probably enjoying time with Jesus during most of the evenings—learning more about our heavenly Father and gaining better insight into the heavenly kingdom. There are some things that we need to examine first to get a better understanding of the responsibility of the Holy Spirit as we move into the friendship mode of the Holy Spirit. Since the Bible says that Jesus was anointed by the Holy Spirit, meaning that He was given ability by the Holy Spirit to do what He did, we must understand that the Holy Spirit is a Person. He has the attributes or qualities that a human being has, so we have to accept the fact that He is able to speak and communicate with us. Jesus referred to the Holy Spirit as a Person—not a thing or feeling, although the more we yield ourselves to His care and influence, the more we understand His human qualities and are more capable of knowing Jesus better. One of the most significant and important things that the Holy Spirit does is reveal Jesus Christ to us. He is the One Who draws and influences us to desire and to know Jesus Christ.

No one is able to come to Me unless the Father Who sent Me attracts and draws him and gives him the desire to come to Me, and (then) I will raise him up (from the dead) at the last day (John 6:44).

Without the influence of the Holy Spirit we cannot be saved, nor can we know Christ intimately. During the times that Jesus spent with His disciples, He became their friends. They learned to love Jesus and to understand the nature of God through observing Him. Of course, when Jesus told them that He was going to be crucified, this caused them great distress and some confusion. In their hearts, they wanted Jesus to remain with them since He had brought them so much victory and joy, and His words, that came from God, had benefited the people so. However, Jesus' purpose for coming was to reveal God Himself to men, giving them the desire to want and follow Him for themselves. This is how Jesus became the Son of mankind. He gave Himself so that we might literally become the sons of God through His death, burial, and resurrection. Let us examine some Scriptures about the Holy Spirit.

As Jesus began to approach the end of His life in this world, He shared this fact with His disciples. Stretch your imagination a bit here. Jesus had told them, perhaps many times, about His purpose on earth—He was the sacrificial Lamb of God who was to take away the sins of the world. But He was not what most expected. The people saw the miracles but the disciples saw Jesus as a confidant, a friend, and a companion, so His telling them that He was leaving them was very distressful.

Do not let your hearts be troubled (distressed, agitated). You believe in and adhere to and trust in and rely on God; believe in and adhere to and trust in and rely also on Me (John 14:1).

Jesus could understand how they were troubled deeply by what He had said earlier during the evening:

Now is the Son of Man glorified! (Now He has achieved His glory, His honor, His exaltation!) And God has been glorified through and in Him...(Dear) little children, I am to be with you only a little longer. You will look for Me and, as I told the Jews, so I tell you now; you are not able to come where I am going...In My Father's house there are many dwelling places (homes). If it were not so, I would have told you; for I am going away to prepare a place for you. And when (if) I go and make ready a place for you, I will come back again and will take you to Myself, that where I am you may be also (John 13:31,33; 14:2-3).

Here we see Jesus telling His disciples that He is going away to be with His Father once again as He was before; however, Jesus took the opportunity to tell His disciples about Someone who was coming in His place. We must understand that if Jesus had not died, the Holy Spirit would have not been able to come and live inside us.

We have been inundated by Hollywood to believe that when a spirit comes into a person, it is an evil spirit. However, what makes us children of God is the fact that we have the Holy Spirit living within us. We are born with a spirit within us; however, we are not alive in our spirits until we accept Jesus Christ as our Savior. Without the impression and influence of the Holy Spirit in our lives, we cannot know and understand God better.

And you (He made alive), when you were dead (slain) by (your) trespasses and sins. In which at one time you walked (habitually). You were following the course and fashion of this world (were under the sway of the tendency of this present age), following the prince of the power of the air. (You were obedient to and under the control of) the (demon) spirit that still constantly works in the sons of disobedience (the careless, the rebellious, and the unbelieving, who go against the purposes of God) (Ephesians 2:1-2).

But God—so rich is He in His mercy! Because of

and in order to satisfy the great and wonderful and intense love with which He loved us, even when we were dead (slain) by (our own) shortcomings and trespasses, He made us alive together in fellowship and in union with Christ; (He gave us the very life of Christ Himself, the same new life with which He quickened Him, for) it is by grace (His favor and mercy which you did not deserve) that you are saved (delivered from judgment and made partakers of Christ's salvation) (Ephesians 2:4-5).

Let us examine the following Scriptures to see the Holy Spirit's desire in our lives.

This is My commandment: that you love one another (just) as I have loved you. No one has greater love (no one has shown stronger affection) than to lay down (give up) his own life for his friends. You are My friends if you keep on doing the things which I command you to do. I do not call you servants (slaves) any longer, for the servant does not know what his master is doing (working out). But I have called you My friends, because I have made known to you everything that I have heard from My Father (I have revealed to you everything that I have learned from Him.) (John 15:12-15).

Father, I desire that they also whom You have entrusted to Me (as Your gift to Me) may be with Me where I am, so that they may see My glory, which You have given Me (Your love gift to Me); for You loved Me before the foundation of the world (John 17:24).

There was never anyone else like Jesus Christ, who not only showed God to us in the body of a man, but revealed the deity of God in the works He did. It was a very sad time when Jesus said that He had to go away. If it was hard for the disciples to let Him go to be crucified, they would obviously have trouble believing that He would return to them. This is where faith takes place. The Scriptures had already foretold what would happen to the Son of God when He came into the world—but most of us often put off what God says as being something for the distant future. The disciples were dumfounded by what seemed sudden to them—their lives were practically ending, as their Friend made it clear that He was leaving them. They did not understand what Jesus was saying until they had actually gone through the time frame of the crucifixion and the actual coming of the Holy Spirit to live within them.

If you (really) love Me, you will keep (obey) My commands. And I will ask the Father, and He will give you another Comforter (Counselor, Helper, Intercessor, Advocate, Strengthener, and Standby), that He may remain with you forever. The Spirit of Truth, Whom the world cannot receive (welcome, take to its heart), because it does not see Him or know and recognize Him. But you know and recognize Him, for He lives with you (constantly) and will be in you. I will not leave you as orphans (comfortless, desolate, bereaved, forlorn, helpless); I will come (back) to you (John 14:15-18).

But the Comforter (Counselor, Helper, Intercessor, Advocate, Strengthener, Standby), the Holy Spirit, Whom the Father will send in My name (in My place) to represent Me and act (on My behalf), He will teach you all things. And He will cause you to recall (will remind you of, bring to your remembrance) everything I have told you (John 14:26).

So we see that the Holy Spirit is a Person. He would live within the disciples. He would remind them of all Jesus said and teach them how Jesus did what He did. The key was being consistently obedient to what Jesus said. This would enable them to consistently enjoy the presence of the Holy Spirit, which is also the key for us to enjoy Him as well.

Before we move on to some other things, let us examine what has been said. It is important that we understand together that Jesus lived as a human being. He lived life in front of His disciples. They ate with Him and talked with Him. Yet even though He performed many miracles with them for many people—even teaching them to do the same thing, they could not separate His humanity from His deity. They experienced heartache in letting Him go, but when the Holy Spirit did come, they understood all that they needed to. It takes time for God to explain things to us so that we may receive insight into His work.

The Holy Spirit is God—His Spirit now living within us. How did we receive God's Spirit? By responding to the Holy Spirit correctly, when we were convicted through hearing the Gospel preached. The Holy Spirit will cause us to believe that Jesus Christ is God's Son. Although we may not understand all this in the initial stages of our salvation, as we continue to abide with the Holy Spirit in prayer, worship, and listening to Him, we will have insight into all things significant, as the Lord leads us.

In th next chapter we will discuss being filled with the Holy Spirit and what that means.

Chapter 8

He Is With Us and in Us

The Spirit of Truth, Whom the world cannot receive (welcome, take to its heart), because it does not see Him or know and recognize Him. But you know and recognize Him, for He lives with you (constantly) and will be in you. I will not leave you as orphans (comfortless, desolate, bereaved, forlorn, helpless); I will come (back) to you (John 14:17-18).

Remembering Scriptures like the above one where Jesus told us about the Holy Spirit is very important. Jesus was God in bodily form. The disciples did not want Him to leave because they had finally recognized Him as God; however, the greatest revelation of Jesus Christ to us today comes through the inner witness we have by the Holy Spirit living within us. All of us have spirits; they are either alive, meaning they respond to Christ because we have believed in Him, accepting Him as our Savior; or they are non-responsive to Him. This means that the person has not accepted Jesus Christ as His Savior. Now, we know because of what Jesus said that we have the Holy Spirit living inside of us, as the above Scripture details.

*But when He, the Spirit of Truth (the Truth-giving
Spirit) comes, He will guide you into all the Truth
(the whole, full Truth). For He will not speak His
own message (on His own authority); but He will
tell whatever He hears (from the Father; He will give
the message that has been given to Him), and He
will announce and declare to you the things that are
to come (that will happen in the future). He will
honor and glorify Me, because He will take of (receive, draw upon) what is Mine and will reveal (declare, disclose, transmit) it to you (John 16:13-14).*

The disciples scattered after Jesus was arrested. This
was just before His crucifixion, which He had predicted.
From Scripture we see that Peter tried to stop Jesus from
fulfilling His destiny—being crucified for the salvation of
mankind. Peter did not know what he was doing. Had we
been in a similar situation, we would have probably done
the same thing.

It was vitally important to the disciples that they had an
understanding of what Jesus meant by saying "He is with
you," meaning, the Holy Spirit, and "He will be in you." Let
us take a look at the incident recorded in Scripture about
the two disciples who were walking along the Emmaus road
after Jesus had been crucified.

*And behold, that very day two of (the disciples)
were going to a village called Emmaus, (which is)
about seven miles from Jerusalem. And they were
talking with each other about all these things that
had occurred. And while they were conversing and
discussing together, Jesus Himself caught up with
them and was already accompanying them. But*

their eyes were held, so that they did not recognize Him. And He said to them, What is this discussion that you are exchanging (throwing back and forth) between yourselves as you walk along? And they stood still, looking sad and downcast. Then one of them, named Cleopas, answered Him, Do you alone dwell as a stranger in Jerusalem and not know the things that have occurred there in these days? And He said to them, What (kind of) things? And they said to Him, About Jesus of Nazareth, Who was a Prophet mighty in work and word before God and all the people—and how our chief priests and rulers gave Him up to be sentenced to death, and crucified Him. But we were hoping that it was He Who would redeem and set Israel free. Yes, and besides all this, it is now the third day since these things occurred (Luke 24:13-21).

If we continue to read we will see how Jesus completely gave witness to what the Scriptures had said about Him. And as He spoke to the two men, their hearts began to believe what was spoken about Him. But we must remember that the entire city was stirred and emotions ran high after such a thing. However, Jesus gave proof and validity to the Scriptures by revealing Himself to the men. Remember, however, He did not reveal Himself until He had shared what the Scriptures had foretold about Him. It was then that the men believed that He was indeed the Christ. Again, Jesus said: "He (meaning, the Holy Spirit) is with you and He will be in you," meaning that He will live within you. But this could have not been possible until Jesus went back to heaven. Before He went to heaven, He instructed the disciples to go to Jerusalem to wait on the promise of the Holy Spirit.

And while being in their company and eating at the table with them, He commanded them not to leave Jerusalem but to wait for what the Father had promised, Of which (He said) you have heard Me speak. (John 14:16, 26; 15:26). For John baptized with water, but not many days from now you shall be baptized with (placed in, introduced into) the Holy Spirit...But you shall receive power (ability, efficiency, and might) when the Holy Spirit has come upon you, and you shall be My witnesses in Jerusalem and all Judea and Samaria and to the ends (the very bounds) of the earth (Acts 1:5,8).

My intention is not that we have an exhaustive study of who the Holy Spirit is, but to show us how He lives with us and helps us. He is the One who introduces us to Jesus Christ and enables us to remain in Him. To be filled with the Holy Spirit simply means to be controlled by Him. I have often heard many people say, "I want more of the Holy Spirit," when in actuality, what they need is to surrender more of themselves to Him. As we yield ourselves to the presence of the Holy Spirit within us, we begin to gain greater insight, depth, and quality experience with who Jesus really was in the earth, and how He walked with God so closely. He undoubtedly had a strong relationship with His Father and imputed this great gift to us. The Holy Spirit responds to faith. If we believe what we already know about God and put that into practice, then the Holy Spirit will fill us and compel us in other areas. Obeying the Lord creates a hunger and thirst within us to desire more of God's Presence and to be controlled by Him.

Blessed and fortunate and happy and spiritually

prosperous (in that state in which the born-again child of God enjoys His favor and salvation) are those who hunger and thirst for righteousness (uprightness and right standing with God), for they shall be completely satisfied! (Matthew 5:6).

This is something that we can practice. Look at the impact that Jesus' resurrection had on His disciples. They actually saw Him after He had been raised from the dead. They had an encounter with Him, fully restored. We must remember they saw how horribly Jesus had been beaten and how He died on the cross. Then suddenly, He appeared to them again as He had promised. This affected their faith level.

In these days, if we obey the Lord—hearing Him, listening to Him in prayer, and exercising our faith in Him— the Holy Spirit produces the same results in us as He did in the first followers of Christ; however, we must respond to Him by faith.

So faith comes by hearing (what is told), and what is heard comes by the preaching (of the message that came from the lips) of Christ (the Messiah Himself) (Romans 10:17).

Now we have full access to our Lord through the Holy Spirit. Jesus showed how the Holy Spirit was still speaking and acting through Him once He was raised from the dead, through speaking with the disciples on the Emmaus road. The Holy Spirit has the same power now as He did then; however, if we are to see such power in our lives, then we do not need to expect more of the Holy Spirit, but yield more of ourselves to Him by accepting and believing Him.

Now as we believe the Holy Spirit, He will demonstrate great power through us. But we must allow Him to be the One who demonstrates. Our main objective in knowing the Holy Spirit better should not be to get power from Him, but so that He can exercise His power within us, giving us the same joy in knowing Christ as the earlier followers did.

As we move forward, I want to share a few examples about what the Scripture says about the Holy Spirit's abiding Presence. If we want to know Christ better—more intimately, then we must know how the Holy Spirit works today. We cannot limit ourselves or the Holy Spirit to Scripture quoting. We must allow the Holy Spirit to speak the words of Christ into our hearts, so that just as the Emmaus road disciples bore witness to the Truth of God inwardly, we may experience the same thing. And as we practice getting to know the Holy Spirit more, we will become more courageous in our walk with Him. Many of the things that we read about in Scripture will begin to take on an altogether different light, as well as coming alive in our hearts today.

Chapter 9

The Influence

We have read in the Book of Acts the wonderful testimonies of those who were impacted and controlled by the Holy Spirit's influence. At this point, I would like to share with us several Scriptures regarding the Holy Spirit. My first desire is to share these references, and then in the next Chapter share some personal experiences that may help us better understand that the Lord is still speaking and directing us today. We must continue to be familiar with the Scriptures, so that when the Holy Spirit is leading us we will know that it is His leadership. And again, it is important to cultivate a relationship with the Holy Spirit. My primary way of enhancing my sensitivity to the Holy Spirit is by acknowledging Him in all things so that I can know when He is trying to get my attention.

Then Jesus was led (guided) by the (Holy) Spirit into the wilderness (desert) to be tempted (tested and tried) by the devil (Matthew 4:1).

Now there was a man in Jerusalem whose name was Simeon, and this man was righteous and de-

*vout (cautiously and carefully observing the divine
Law), and looking for the Consolation of Israel; and
the Holy Spirit was upon him. And it had been divinely revealed (communicated) to him by the Holy
Spirit that he would not see death before he had
seen the Lord's Christ (the Messiah, the Anointed
One). And prompted by the (Holy) Spirit, he came
into the temple (enclosure); and when the parents
brought in the little child Jesus to do for Him what
was customary according to the Law, (Simeon)
took Him up in his arms and praised and thanked
God and said, And now, Lord, You are releasing
Your servant to depart (leave this world) in peace,
according to Your word. For with my (own) eyes I
have seen Your Salvation (Luke 2:25-30).*

*So he got up and went. And behold, an Ethiopian, a
eunuch of great authority under Candace the queen
of the Ethiopians, who was in charge of all her treasure, had come to Jerusalem to worship. And he
was (now) returning, and sitting in his chariot he
was reading the book of the prophet Isaiah. Then
the (Holy) Spirit said to Philip, Go forward and join
yourself to this chariot (Acts 8:27-28).*

The Spirit of the Lord God is upon me... (Isaiah
61:1).

It will be of great advantage to continue reading the
Scriptures to see how the Lord speaks and leads His people.
Many people find it difficult to believe that we can be led so
clearly by the Lord. My objective in this writing is not to try
and convince you that the Holy Spirit still speaks to us but

to get you to exercise your rights given you as a believer. Now, a believer is not only an individual who has accepted Jesus Christ, but one who continues to believe Christ in action. We are told to be doers of God's word, but we must also understand that if we are to see the power and effectiveness that Jesus saw, we must be led by the Holy Spirit.

> *So Jesus answered them by saying, I assure you, most solemnly I tell you, the Son is able to do nothing of Himself (of His own accord); but He is able to do only what He sees the Father doing, for whatever the Father does is what the Son does in the same way (in His turn)* (John 5:19).

Hearing the Father Speak

We must understand that as a result of Jesus complete sacrifice in this world, we are now able to hear our Father speak to us by the indwelling presence of the Holy Spirit. Jesus was able to hear His Father speak inwardly and obeyed what He was told.

I would strongly suggest that if we want to cultivate this beautiful gift and ability that Christ has afforded us, we should practice it every day. How do we know that the Holy Spirit is able to lead and guide us? Practice. How do we know that the Holy Spirit can speak to us and shows personal interest in our lives? We simply begin acknowledging Him, believing that He is the Person whom Jesus promised that would come to live within us—just as He did with Jesus.

From the Scripture reference in Acts 8, we can see that the Holy Spirit was able to speak to Philip so that He could lead him in the right direction to accomplish an eternal purpose within the Ethiopian. One of the ways that we can genuinely see the Holy Spirit at work in us today is allowing Him liberty to work.

We must remember that the Holy Spirit is a Person. He is capable of understanding us and revealing things to us. He is capable of loving and being compassionate. All of the characteristics that Jesus possessed are in the Person of the Holy Spirit.

We can see by Simeon in Matthew that he was led to the Temple at the exact time that Jesus would be there. This means that Simeon had to have been in fellowship with the Holy Spirit for quite some time. Anyone who can be led so clearly by the Holy Spirit had to have been cultivating a relationship with Him all along.

Yielding to God

But how was it possible for Old Testament men and women to hear and recognize God so well? Take Abraham, for instance. We must accept that Abraham's attention was gotten by God and Abraham obeyed God. Because Abraham obeyed God, He was afforded insight into God's plan. The key here is not so much whether or not the Old Testament saints had the Holy Spirit living with them, they paid attention to what God was speaking to them—giving themselves to God as He gave them instruction. They were yielding their lives to Him as He communicated with their spirits. *We must understand that God was able to speak to their spirits because they yielded themselves to Him.* Here, I would like to share an example with you.

I am a shopper. I enjoy buying nice clothes. I remember once going to a store where I saw a very nice shirt. I wanted to buy the shirt but then saw how expensive it was. I was tempted to go ahead and get the shirt, but then I thought of asking the Lord to lead me back to the store when the shirt was on sale.

Now, sometimes when I have gone shopping I have had the money to buy what I wanted but decided that the asking price was too much. There is a difference in spending the money and getting what you want and not spending the money because you are afraid that you will not have money later for some unforeseen problem. (I will share a little bit about that later.) But this time I believed that the Lord would lead me back to the store at the right time to get the shirt on sale.

Now, is it spiritual for us to ask the Lord to lead us to where sales are? Well, if the Lord has promised to clothe us, then I am sure that He does not object to us asking Him to lead us to places to find what we like as well as where the prices are reasonable.

I had just about forgotten about the shirt until one day I was in the store and simply felt led to look for the shirt. I believe in my heart that the Holy Spirit had led me to the store and was now leading me to buy the shirt. It had been quite sometime since I first saw the shirt, and surely, I thought, it would be gone by now.

I saw a clearance rack in front of me and began looking on it for the shirt. I saw the shirt right away, which had been marked down about $30, but it wasn't in my size so I kept looking. Finally, I saw the shirt again, and I felt the Holy Spirit saying it was alright to get it. This is exactly what I had wanted, and the Holy Spirit led me to get the shirt at the right time.

Some might read this testimony and wonder if it is right to ask God to lead us to things. I have found that as I have asked the Lord to lead me, practicing this as often as I can,

He orders my steps and leads me directly to what I want. This process has caused me to be able to see Jesus more clearly in everyday life and to walk with a grateful heart.

> *Up to this time you have not asked a (single) thing in My Name (as presenting all that I Am); but now ask and keep on asking and you will receive, so that your joy (gladness, delight) may be full and complete* (John 16:24).

> *The steps of a (good) man are directed and established by the Lord when He delights in his way (and He busies Himself with his every step)* (Psalm 37:23).

> *In all your ways know, recognize, and acknowledge Him, and He will direct and make straight and plain your paths* (Proverbs 3:6).

I have found that if I will acknowledge the Holy Spirit— not necessarily praying, but simply accepting the fact that He is with me, He will lead me. Sometimes this influence may come in the form of a thought, impression or feeling. But again, we must remember that if we consider Him and acknowledge Him, the Holy Spirit will reveal Himself to us in various ways.

Intimacy is what the Holy Spirit desires with and from us. As we continue to recognize Him, welcome Him, embrace and believe Him, He will show us things that we cannot know on our own. Jesus promised that He would show us things that are to come. Now, if we believe that He is able to do such things, our lives will become more exciting concerning spiritual things.

Personally, I have found my life to be more fun as I yield myself to the Lord more. I have not found this very difficult to do as time has passed. Actually, I have found life far less stressful by seeking to know the Holy Spirit better. As we continue to seek and see Him operating in our lives, we will grow to love Jesus more.

In the next chapter, I will share how what is important to us is important to Him.

Chapter 10

The Lord Will Lead

The Lord is my Shepherd (to feed, guide, and shield me), I shall not lack (Psalm 23:1).

In the previous chapter I mentioned how I enjoyed shopping, and how I prayed that the Holy Spirit would lead me back to a certain store when a shirt went on sale. Once the Lord did this for me, it caused me to want to do this kind of thing more often. But we must understand that this was an area that I liked and with which I was comfortable. There are times when the Lord will require us to spend what we may feel that we do not have to get what we want. Let me explain from experience.

Some years ago I remember needing a winter coat because the weather was changing, and it was getting colder. I had put some money in what I will call a hidden place in my wallet. Well, one evening I was sitting at home and the Holy Spirit spoke to me.

"Larry, I know where there is a coat, and you will certainly like it."

"Really," I thought, and then I became excited about getting the coat. Because I was beginning to really hear God better, I was also beginning to trust Him. Each time He had spoken to me about going to a certain place or doing a certain thing, I felt more confident and certain that I would find what I was looking for. But when He spoke to me about it, I considered the amount of money that I had, not really counting the money that I had hidden in my wallet. I had determined that money was for a rainy day.

Once the Lord spoke to me about the coat, I knew immediately in my heart where to go and look for it. Now, this may bring a few questions to mind. How did I know that I was just going to look for a coat? Suppose I did not find what I was looking for? What if I did see a coat and liked it but did not have the money for it? Suppose I was being deceived into thinking that I was hearing from the Lord?

All of these are valid questions. From my experience with the Lord, He speaks His Word to me. It is not like Scriptures being quoted. When the Holy Spirit speaks the Word of God to my spirit, the words come alive. In my mind I can sometimes see exactly where I'm supposed to go and what I am supposed to do.

So Jesus answered them by saying, I assure you, most solemnly I tell you, the Son is able to do nothing of Himself (of His own accord); but He is able to do only what He sees the Father doing, for whatever the Father does is what the Son does in the same way (in His turn) (John 5:19).

Now, if we are sincerely learning to know God better, then He will better acquaint Himself with us through things that are important to us—things that mean something to us in this life. Things are important and we need them. And if we can see how well God leads us to get the things we need in life, then He will soon be able to trust us in other areas to hear Him and then follow His leading. Trust is something that is earned and secured as two people get to know each other.

The Leading of the Holy Spirit

We must also believe that the Holy Spirit is able to lead us. He is a Person, and Jesus told us that He would lead us into all truth. Since this is the case, then we must believe that the Holy Spirit is able to show us where things are that we need and to tell us how to get there. Granted, this is a learning process that takes time.

As I share with you some more intimate details of how the Lord has led me, be sure to think about some times how the Lord has led you. If you have to, go back to those places where you were sure the Lord was speaking to you and use them as a launching pad for how the Lord may desire to lead you now. It is wise to practice ways that the Lord leads you. Practice speaking to the Lord out loud as you can, expecting Him to speak back, just as any friend would speak to us. God has indeed called us His friend.

Now we must know for certain that Jesus had needs when He was in this world. Of course He did, we all do. Jesus knew, however, how to get His needs met. He trusted His heavenly Father, and He practiced what to do in front of His disciples, teaching and training them how to exercise their faith. We know that faith comes by hearing and hearing by the Word of God, or what the Holy Spirit is speaking to us from the Scriptures. Here are two examples of how God provided for the needs of those who followed Jesus.

However, in order not to give offense and cause

them to stumble (that is, to cause them to judge un-favorably and unjustly) go down to the sea and throw in a hook. Take the first fish that comes up, and when you open its mouth you will find there a shekel. Take it and give it to them to pay the temple tax for Me and for yourself (Matthew 17:27).

Now it occurred that while the people pressed upon Jesus to hear the message of God, He was standing by the Lake of Gennesaret (Sea of Galilee). And He saw two boats drawn up by the lake, but the fish-ermen had gone down from them and were washing their nets. And getting into one of the boats, (the one) that belonged to Simon (Peter), He requested him to draw away a little from the shore. Then He sat down and continued to teach the crowd (of people) from the boat. When He had stopped speaking, He said to Simon (Peter), Put out into the deep (water), and lower your nets for a haul. And Simon (Peter) answered, Master, we toiled all night (exhaustingly) and caught nothing (in our nets). But on the ground of Your word, I will lower the nets (again). And when they had done this, they caught a great number of fish; and as their nets were (at the point of) breaking, they sig-naled to their partners in the other boat to come and take hold with them. And they came and filled both the boats, so that they began to sink (Luke 5:1-7).

We know that fish cannot use money, so why would there be one who had some in its mouth? How could Jesus have known about the fish carrying money in its mouth? He saw it because it had been revealed to Him by God. Jesus knew the exact thing to do to get the fish and pay His taxes. Now, the miracle was not so much for Jesus as it was His disciple.

Secondly, we see so many fish being caught that the disciples' boats almost sank. What was miraculous was that it was at a time of day when fish do not bite as well. We also see that the disciples had given up fishing for the day—but at Jesus' command, they went out. Let's examine how Jesus first borrowed Peter's boat. Once He was finished using Peter's boat, Jesus blessed him by performing a miracle that blessed his livelihood. Peter made his living by fishing. He was a fisherman. The point that we must see is that what is important to us is important also to God. He cares about our personal existence. And as we walk with Him, He will demonstrate this in varying ways; however, we must trust Him. As I said earlier, trust is something that is developed. Sometimes, the Lord may stretch us a bit in our relationship with Him, proving that He still has our best interests at heart. Whenever God stretches us, it is always intended to make us stronger in our faith. As our faith grows stronger, we are better able to see our Lord do greater things for us as well as others.

When I got to the store where I had felt led to buy the coat, I was very excited. I knew in my heart that there would be a coat and that I would like it. Every time I have felt led of the Holy Spirit to get something, I feel so alive.

There it was! It was beautiful. I mean, it was everything that I had wanted in a coat. The color was perfect, and it fit perfectly too. When I tried it on it was a light jacket but it was very warm—perfect for what I liked. But then I looked at the price.

"Oh," I said. I was a bit disappointed, because I did not have enough money in my pocket.

"What's wrong?" The Holy Spirit asked.

"Nothing," I said, not wanting to readily admit that I did not have the money.

"Don't you like the color?" He asked.

"Yes," I said.

"Then what is wrong?" He asked.

There I stood holding the coat in my hands, not wanting to tell the Lord that I did not have the money.

"I don't have the money," I finally admitted.

"What's that hidden in your wallet?" He asked, but I did not want to spend it. I was saving it for a rainy day, not realizing that it was raining at that present moment.

"You remind Me of the children of Israel," the Lord said to me. "They did not trust Me, either."

Before I write any further, I must tell you that I did not feel condemned by what the Lord said to me, but I honestly felt convicted. I also felt that I had saddened Him by not believing that He would replace, if necessary, the money that I would spend on the jacket. So I do not want to misrepresent Him in anyway by sharing what He said.

"Put it back on the shelf and go home," He said. By this time I felt really terrible. I really wanted that coat, but was afraid to buy it, thinking that it would take all the money I had.

I did not have a pleasant time once I got home. I was very upset because I had left the jacket in the store. I felt so terrible that I went to bed before it was completely dark outside. Even then, the Holy Spirit was still dealing with me.

"Larry," He said. "Money is meant to serve you. Don't you serve it. Go back and get the jacket that you want. You will be fine." Once I heard Him speak this to my heart, I felt better—much better. I understood then that the Lord wanted me to trust Him for what I needed with what I had. I also understood that He was teaching me to trust Him and not what I had in my pocket. God is faithful.

As we live our lives with God, He will challenge us in areas. The more we believe and respond favorably to Him, the more He will use us for greater purposes. It is not that we are striving for greater works or purposes, but we are pressing inward to know our heavenly Father better.

> *But in a great house there are not only vessels of gold and silver, but also (utensils) of wood and earthen ware, and some for honorable and noble (use) and some for menial and ignoble (use). So whoever cleanses himself (from what is ignoble and unclean, who separates himself from contact with contaminating and corrupting influences) will (then himself) be a vessel set apart and useful for honorable and noble purposes, consecrated and profitable to the Master, fit and ready for any good work (2 Timothy 2:20-21).*

Chapter 11

Signs and Wonders

I was born and raised in Alabama. I grew up among a number of my relatives that lived on a single street, named after ourselves. The rural area was one where people knew each other, and seldom did you hear about crime in this small place. In fact, I cannot think of a single crime that was reported during all these years. But I am sure that just as I have changed, things have changed in that small town that I called home for some 20 odd years.

When I lived in Alabama I worked for ten years at a textile factory. I know that may sound like a lot of time, and it is, now that I think about it. This was the second job that I had gotten, and my Dad was responsible for putting in a good word for me where he worked. It turned out that I was hired shortly after I'd entered high school.

It was during the later years of my employment at this company that I recognized Jesus Christ as my Savior. I was always what some would call a good kid, but during those times people were just better natured than they are now, or so it seems. Some even found it hard to believe when I began to talk about Jesus a lot, often saying, "I thought you were already a Christian." But I did not really know the

Lord up until my mid-twenties. I came to the altar when I was thirteen years old, but as we grow older things change. We become independent, or so we think and begin desiring to leave our roots. But this was not altogether the case for me. I did not want to leave my hometown or my friends and family, but the more I grew to know the Lord, the more I felt His leading me somewhere else—but I did not quite know where at the time. The Lord has a way of dealing with us inwardly. He can speak to us in every place, whether we are alone or in a crowded room. He has the ability to isolate us, getting our attention. And because we know that His Spirit lives within us, we can also feel sad when He is sad. I learned that this sadness sometimes has to do with what His plans are and whether or not we are following them.

I want to share with you that I sincerely loved my home town. Some would say that it was much like Mayberry. The people were friendly, and somehow it seemed as if I'd be there forever. But then I began to hear from the Lord regularly enough to know that change was coming. I could feel it. As I am writing this I am reminded of what my pastor told me some years ago. He said: "Brother Reese, you won't be here long," speaking of the church. "You love Jesus too much, and anyone who loves Jesus as much as you do does not stay in one place long." I now know what he meant. Those words of his have followed and supported me for many years.

I remember when the Lord began to speak with me about leaving home—my family, my job, my friends, my everything. Everything that had become familiar, the Lord was now requiring me to give it up. I felt it inside, but I did not want to accept the idea. It was something that I found comfortable running away from. We read in Scripture how the Lord required His people to give up their very lives, but it is different somehow, when He begins to make it personal. As I ignored what I felt in my heart, I felt even sadder. The feeling suggested that I would not be where I was long. I was able to tell what He was feeling. And because I was yielding myself to Him so often, I could not help but feel this deep tugging at my heart, saying, "You will not be here long."

"I am sending you away from your family," the Lord spoke to me one day, very clearly. "Yes, I am sending you away." When I heard Him the second time, I semi-surrendered my heart to Him. Yes, I heard Him. Yes, I wanted to obey Him because I loved Him deeply, but I was afraid to comply. Questions began to come into my mind about what I would do, where I would go, where would I work, and how would I survive—all of which are valid questions. I had never left my relatives before and was still what I would consider very young in the Lord. I needed time. I needed to be sure that it was the Lord. But in my heart I knew that it was Father. I knew that it was His voice that I was hearing. I felt it long before He ever spoke one word. Sometimes, God does not always permit us to get ready to do what He is speaking to us.

Being intimate means being able to share your heart—finding out what someone else is thinking and being able to say what you feel without being afraid. I felt this way towards the Lord. I believed that I could share my heart openly with Him, even if I wanted to complain.

As we talk to the Lord regularly, we learn how to speak with Him. We learn His feelings. We begin to know how He feels as we discuss things with Him. Clearly, we learn to know Him intimately as He deals with us about what is significant and important to us. And my family was the dearest thing to me.

"I don't know if I can do this," I told Him. I remember

walking outside one of the textile plants when the Lord began to speak with me about what I was concerned. He wants to know our feelings. In sharing our hearts with our heavenly Father, we begin to expect His answers. They may not always be what we want them to be, but we must learn to be inquisitive rather than critical. We must learn to ask God what He desires and to depend on Him to show us how to carry out His plans. The Lord will not always tell us all the details, but He will give us enough insight to sustain us. This is where our faith comes into play. When God speaks to us, we have the right or privilege as His children to respond with questions. He will sometimes speak to us those things that are impossible or highly improbable; however, when He speaks, what seems impossible and improbable becomes possible.

> *And the angel said to her, Do not be afraid, Mary, for you have found grace (free, spontaneous, absolute favor and loving-kindness) with God. And listen! You will become pregnant and will give birth to a Son, and you shall call His name Jesus.... And Mary said to the angel, How can this be, since I have no (intimacy with any man as a) husband? Then the angel said to her, The Holy Spirit will come upon you....* (Luke 1:30,34-35).

Here we see that Mary asked questions of the angel, and even though He told her how Jesus would be born, she did not understand. Nothing had ever been told her personally by God before, but we see that it was proven to be true later.

"I know that this is hard on you," the Holy Spirit spoke to me as I walked along the sidewalk. "But you must leave from among your family."

"Why," I asked, hoping that the Lord would change His mind, but knowing that He would not.

"I have plans for you, Larry, and your family does not believe Me the way that you do. Your faith is strong and you are growing into the person I have called you to be. Therefore, I will be leading you away to that which is not familiar, so that I might train you and that you may know that I am the Lord."

"Father, I want to obey you. I sincerely do because I love you. But this is hard. Really, this is hard for me. I mean, this is all that I know." Looking around me as I continued to walk, I looked up into the trees along the sidewalk and wondered how I could do such a thing as leave the family. How could I explain to them what I was doing? Would they understand? Then it dawned on me that my dad would not understand. Here I had worked all these years and was now leaving, not sure where I would work or make a living to wherever the Lord was sending me.

"I know that this is hard on you," the Lord said. "But it is what I have designed for you. I will be with you. You will not be alone. I know that you want to obey Me, and I will give you some time, as this is something I have not asked of you to do before."

"But Lord, who did you ever ask to leave home, their relatives?" I asked. Bear in mind that during this time I was a growing Christian and did not know much about the Scriptures.

"Abraham," the Lord said. "Read about Abraham." Once I heard this, I felt much better.

"Thank you, Lord," I said, complying with what He was speaking, but I was still very concerned about what my dad would say. Just the fresh revelation of hearing that I would be leaving my home town was news enough for one day, and basically all that I could handle. I would wait to ask the Lord about how to speak with my dad later.

Now (in Haran) the Lord said to Abram, go for yourself (for your own advantage) away from your country, from your relatives and your father's house, to the land that I will show you... (Genesis 12:1).

Chapter 12

Talk and Listen

In my distress (when seemingly closed in) I called upon the Lord and cried to my God; He heard my voice out of His temple (heavenly dwelling place), and my cry came before Him into His (very) ears (Psalm 18:6).

I will confess, praise, and give thanks to You, for You have heard and answered me, and You have become my Salvation and Deliverer (Psalm 118:21).

Now, if we are going to walk with God and become more intimately acquainted with Him, we will eventually have to learn to communicate to others what God is saying. This is not always necessary because some things our Father speaks to us are for us alone; however, He will require us to tell others certain things from time to time. During those times our confidence levels will be high and strong if we listen to God so that He can tell us what to say and how to say it. We do not go around looking for things to tell people from God. We always want to be encouragers, bringing encouraging things to people, but I have learned that whatever

75

God says can be viewed as encouraging, especially as we grow to know Him more intimately.

I have mentioned how I felt about leaving home. One of the hindrances that I faced was speaking to my dad. It was not that my dad was a strict, domineering type; he just had a way about him that was no nonsense. My dad was also a very witty person. I did not know how he would respond to my telling him that God was telling me to leave home. He cared for all of his children deeply, and would first want to know exactly where I was going and if I had work when I got there. If I could satisfactorily answer these questions, I believe he would have no problem with my leaving. After all, these questions made sense, especially to a parent.

Thinking about it now, I was well into my twenties and I should have not been afraid of what my dad had to say about my leaving. I was an adult; however, the Lord was heavily dealing with me to speak with my dad. Now, my mother already knew that I would be leaving. The Lord had already placed these thoughts in her heart. But she did not know altogether where I would go. At least, she never mentioned it to me. I had peace in my heart concerning her but the fear of God was on me regarding telling my dad.

"What am I going to tell him?" I asked the Lord. "What do I say?" I paced the floor of my room, waiting to hear what the Lord would say to me. It was getting closer and closer to the time for me to leave, and I needed to tell my dad. It seemed that I was more afraid of him than the Lord. "He won't understand," I told the Lord.

I remember the soft light that I first saw when I was in the hotel. Remember when I mentioned how the Lord spoke to me in the hotel, asking me to forgive my friends who had hurt me? Well, as I finally sat beside my bed on the floor, I felt His presence in the room in the same way. It was comforting, and my frustration began to leave.

"Lord, what am I going to tell my dad? He won't believe that I have heard from You, and he will try to stop me from leaving," I told Him. "Eventually, I will have to leave, but I want him to be alright with it."

Listening to God

"He will be fine," the Lord told me. It is during these times that I began to really try and silence my mind and pay attention to the Lord. When the Lord speaks to you and you know beyond any question that it is His voice and presence that is with you, pay close attention. Listen to what He has to say—talk, yes, but listen as well. Our heavenly Father wants us to be able to communicate with others what He is sharing with us, but we have to listen fully to what He says, otherwise the message will come across as confusing. Jesus had completely been able to represent His Father to the disciples by simply saying what God had told Him to do.

> I have manifested Your Name (I have revealed Your very Self, Your real Self) to the people whom You have given Me out of the world. They were Yours, and You gave them to Me, and they have obeyed and kept Your word......For the (uttered) words that You gave Me I have given them; and they have received and accepted (them) and have come to know positively and in reality (to believe with absolute assurance) that I came forth from Your presence, and they have believed and are convinced that You did send Me (John 17:6,8).

We are instructed by the Lord to really honor our parents, and I wanted to honor my dad, but somehow I felt that he would not believe that God was sending me away from home. We must know that God knows everything and He knows everyone, so His wisdom is given to us in times when we are afraid; that is, if we will listen to Him. The perfect love of God is seen in how He deals with us—He honors us by giving to us what we do not know on our own, so that we can better enjoy this life. God wants us to enjoy life, not struggle through fears that rob us of that joy.

"I know what your father is like," the Lord said to me. "I know him well. I created him, and I know what he likes even better than you." This was consoling.

"Then you know how I feel," I said.

"Yes, I do." The Lord's voice was calm and I began to further calm down as I listened and rested in His presence. "I am giving you instructions," the Lord said, "not commands. You love Me," He said, "and your heart desires to honor Me. I will teach you what to say to your father. Don't be afraid."

God wants us to get to know Him. If we are to know Him intimately, then we must allow Him to deal with what we are afraid of.

The Love of God

The Bible teaches us some things about the love of God.

And we know (understand, recognize, are conscious of, by observation and by experience) and believe (adhere to and put faith in and rely on) the love God cherishes for us. God is love, and he who dwells and continues in love dwells and continues in God, and God dwells and continues in him.... There is no fear in love (dread does not exist), but full-grown (complete, perfect) love turns fear out of doors and expels every trace of terror! For fear brings with it the thought of punishment, and (so) he who is afraid has not reached the full maturity of love (is not yet grown into love's complete perfection). We love Him, because He first loved us (1 John 4:16,18-19).

As we grow to know how much God loves us, then we are better able to know how much He loves everyone. And if we know how much God loves people, we want to communicate Him to others just the way He has communicated Himself to us, and that is in love.

"Your father knows that you have common sense, Larry," the Lord told me, setting my emotions more at ease. "He trusts you and believes in you. I know that he has not told you these things, but it is the truth."

"Why hasn't he said anything to me?" I asked.

"Some things he cannot say, but he will support you. Just because he has not told you, does not mean that these things are not so. Larry, you do not talk to your father the way that you should, and perhaps that is another reason why you do not know these things. It is I, the Lord, calling you away from home. As I said to you, I have created you for My very own purpose. Once you tell your father that I, the Lord, am sending you away from home, he will accept it. Now, he may ask you some questions; if so, then give him the answers that I, Myself, will give to you."

"Lord, you have told me that I am going to a certain city, but where will I work? You know my dad, and you know he will want to know this probably above anything else. Where will I work?"

"Where do you want to work?" the Lord asked. "What do you want to do?"

"Well...." I was at a loss for words. In my heart a desire

floated to the surface to sell clothes. This had been a desire of mine for years, but I did not believe that I would do it because I had never been hired when I had tried.

"What do you want to do?" The Lord asked me once again. "What is in your heart?" As He settled and calmed my fears, I felt such deep love and concern coming from Him. If we will allow our heavenly Father, He will love us deeply, revealing to us things that bless our hearts. His greatest desire is that we know Him personally, just the way Jesus did. So as we continue to approach Him in prayer, be quiet, listen, then let us adjust our lives to His words, and not our fears.

Let be and be still, and know (recognize and understand) that I am God... (Psalm 46:10).

Delight yourself also in the Lord and He will give you the desires and secret petitions of your heart (Psalm 37:4).

God Reveals Truths About Ourselves

Being intimately acquainted with God also affords Him the ability to tell us the truth about ourselves. The things we fear will always control us unless the Lord is able to reveal the truth to us about what we fear and why we fear those things. Clearly, I was afraid to talk with my dad because I did not feel he would believe the Lord had spoken to me. I wanted him to be proud of me. I did not want him to feel that I was losing my mind and going off to destroy myself.

"Tell him that you will be working in a men's clothing store," the Lord told me. "Is this what you want to do?"

"Yes," I told the Lord, "But I have not applied to a clothing store, Lord. How can this happen?"

"I will see to it that it happens, as you obey Me. I do not want you to be afraid, now. When you go and tell your father that I, the Lord, have told you to leave home, then he will let you go."

Once the Lord said this to me, He stopped speaking to me concerning it. I was left now to share with my dad what He had told me.

I remember the day I went to tell my dad what the Lord had spoken to me about leaving. He was lying on the sofa. I came in quietly as he laid there and sat in a chair opposite to the sofa.

"Daddy, there is something I have to tell you," I said, somehow unafraid, but just a little nervous. He continued to lie quietly, never sitting up.

"The Lord is leading me to leave home...."

I simply told him the things the Lord had told me, and he did not say one word at that time. Somehow as I spoke the words that the Lord had given me, his facial expression said: "I know." And that was all that I needed to see. Somehow, in my heart, I knew that he knew the word was coming from the Lord.

Before I actually left home, he did talk to me about leaving, but he did not try to stop me. As we talk together more about walking in intimacy with our Father, I will share things that I believe affect all of us in life in one way or the other.

Chapter 13

Guide Me

It did not take me a long time to believe that the Lord wanted me to leave home. As I said earlier, the hardest part was speaking to my dad about it. Most of my worry about this was in vain. Once I told him what the Lord had put in my heart, he simply believed me. He did ask a few questions, as any parent would, but he knew that I was good at making decisions and honored what I felt was in my heart to do from the Lord.

Before I left home I had been communicating with some people in the city where the Lord was sending me. It was about a two-hour drive from where I lived, but far enough away from the familiar. The people had been working with me on getting a job in selling clothes, and everything looked very promising. I was at peace about the decision, and it seemed the Lord had helped me make it through the anxiety and sadness that was associated in leaving my family.

Naturally, it felt as if I was being taken away from my family forever, but I felt that the Lord was drawing me closer to Himself. I felt safe. I did not feel alone. But I knew that I had to obey the voice and Spirit of God within. This is how I began to learn to hear and walk with God. He would speak to me in various ways—but mostly, I heard His voice speaking within, and soon, I began to feel what the Lord felt. God's words and thoughts are the same, and thoughts create feelings. As we walk with the Lord, our feelings begin to become His. I am not promoting that we should be led by what we feel; however, I am advocating that feelings are a part of the thought process in obeying God's commands. Familiarity with God's thoughts will reveal His feelings, and passionate feelings are a part of following God's heart.

I had grown accustomed to listening to His inner voice. Listening to God so closely—or developing an inner ear is a very powerful thing. The more we listen to God, the more He will instruct us—giving us instructions to obey—and then confirm what we do with signs and wonders. In other words, what we are hearing inwardly, through our faith in Him, God begins to reveal outwardly. Now when I say signs and wonders, I am not necessarily talking about miracles—but things that confirm outwardly what we hear our heavenly Father speaking about inwardly. For instance, the Lord had told me that I would have a job in retail clothing sales when I moved to this city. At first this really concerned me. I did tell my dad what the Lord said, but since I did not have the job beforehand, I felt as if I had lied to my Dad when I told him. The Lord assured me that I had not lied to my dad, but told him what I had heard from Him. Again, the more we obey the Lord, the more He will reveal Himself. God reveals Himself and becomes acquainted with us through His Word and by His Word. That is why it is important to meditate on what God says. His Words must go beyond our mental understanding, penetrating us inwardly.

But his delight and desire are in the law of the Lord,
and on His law (the precepts, the instructions, the

teachings of God) he habitually meditates (ponders and studies) by day and by night (Psalm 1:2).

And I will give them one heart (a new heart) and I will put a new spirit within them; and I will take the stony (unnaturally hardened) heart out of their flesh, and will give them a heart of flesh (sensitive and responsive to the touch of their God), that they may walk in My statutes and keep My ordinances, and do them. And they shall be My people, and I will be their God (Ezekiel 11:19-20).

I have found that God wants me to talk to Him about what I feel. He does want us to be able to hear His instructions inwardly, but communion and intimacy with God comes from being able to better understand and to respond to Him. God is not upset or angry with us when we ask questions. He wants us to ask questions so that we can gain insight into His divine nature. As we obey God, we are honoring Him, and in honoring Him we are also honored by Him.

Admittedly, in the earlier stages of getting to know the Lord, I sometimes felt as if I was being driven—following commands that I heard coming from God. I did not feel the love that I wanted to feel from God, because I was only concerned with following His instructions. As I have walked with Him these years, I have found that God does want me to obey Him because obedience causes me to understand His ways better as well as causes me to love Him more. Also, it must be understood that we have lived so long not knowing how to obey God. So in the elementary stages, He has to lead us by what seems to be a bit and bridle because we do not know where we are going. Although this kind of control is uncomfortable, it is necessary. Otherwise, we will continue to abort and miss the divine purpose and plan of God. God reveals His love to us as we obey Him. As we continue in obedience, the Lord moves in closer—or becomes more intimately acquainted and involved in our lives. It is then that we see how personal our heavenly Father is and how He wants to share our lives with us. Yes, at first, it may seem that God is giving commands that seem a bit cold— but that is to the untrained ear. However, continuing in our relationship with Him, we begin to see that our heavenly Father is also saying,

"Tell Me what is in your heart. I really want to know." This may come as a surprise to us at first, hearing our heavenly Father respond this way. However, intimacy involves being able to share what you feel—even if you believe it is wrong—even if you believe it is something that the Father may be upset about, if you speak it.

Learning to live this eternal life that we have is far more than studying the Bible. It is engaging personally with the One who gave us His Word as well as His Son, being able to hear Him in all areas of our lives. This kind of walking with God will involve risks to our personal security. This does not mean that our heavenly Father will cause us to be insecure. He will require us to go through what I will call divine discipline so that we will not put our trust in anything but Him. The Scriptures tell us that our Father is a jealous God. Honestly, He can afford to be. He gives us everything that is needed in this life. And as we grow to see this by walking with Him, we will not want anything else. Since God knows us so well, He is able to give us things that bring deep satisfaction inwardly so that we will not want anything that could potentially harm us.

It is important to communicate your heart with Father.

Let Him know when you are upset. Tell Him when you feel disappointed. Where we see only part of the picture before us, the Father sees the entire picture—revealing to us what is necessary, so that we can continue living by faith. Remember, without faith it is impossible to please God. As the Father leads us, try to begin seeing His guiding hand and voice as a means of discipline, instructing us, even though sometimes we may not like it. But God's purpose in divine discipline is to enable us to enjoy Him more.

> *My son, do not think lightly or scorn to submit to the correction and discipline of the Lord, nor lose courage and give up and faint when you are reproved or corrected by Him: for the Lord corrects and disciplines everyone whom He loves, and He punishes, even scourges, every son whom He accepts and welcomes to His heart and cherishes* (Hebrews 12:5-6).

> *For the time being no discipline brings joy, but seems grievous and painful; but afterwards it yields a peaceable fruit of righteousness to those who have been trained by it (a harvest of fruit which consists in righteousness—in conformity to God's will in purpose, thought, and action, resulting in right living and right standing with God)* (Hebrews 12:11).

If we want to feel God's love—sincerely feel it deep within, then we will grow in this as we participate with Him—engaging in divinely appointed exercises. When I knew that the Lord was leading me away from home, I felt punished in ways. I did not know that part of this divinely appointed exercise was to help me know and depend on Him better.

"I must get you away from the influence of the familiar," He had told me. And at that time, He offered no further explanation.

"But I do not understand," I had told Him.

"Obedience will bring understanding," He had said. But I longed to hear Him speaking more lovingly and kind to me. I was giving things up, and it seemed for a time, that He was forcing me to give them up. But I did not know Him like He wanted me to know Him at this point. If we want to know the love of God, then we do not work *for* Him—we work *alongside* Him. When we see that we are a partner with God, working with us so that we can enjoy life better, we begin to break within—becoming more sensitive and sensible to His moving in our lives. As we are better able to see this, we begin to see that He is not taking anything from us, but adding things to us—not only things, but a deeper love for Himself, ourselves as well as others.

We are assured and know that (God being a partner in their labor) all things work together and are (fitting into a plan) for good to and for those who love God and are called according to (His) design and purpose. For those whom He foreknew (of whom He was aware and loved beforehand), He also destined from the beginning (foreordaining them) to be molded into the image of His Son (and share inwardly His likeness), that He might become the firstborn among many brethren (Romans 8:28-29).

Obedience is not a dirty word. But until we begin to develop a relationship with our heavenly Father, it may seem to be. It is so important that our hearing be changed and adjusted. Obeying our heavenly Father consists of more than receiving and obeying orders. Although we may not see it in the beginning, our obedience to God creates within us the ability to hear Him better and to understand Him better. Once we begin to understand our heavenly Father better, He will be able to share with us anything in a Father son relationship, and not in what feels like an us and God relationship. But first He must acquire our attention, leading us away from whatever controls or consumes us. Now this may not be a physical move like the Father required of me. It may simply be a wooing process done by the Holy Spirit, so that we can learn to trust God. As we move forward to the next chapter I will share what happens when it seems that God lets us down.

Chapter 14

Let Him Lead

Do not fret or have any anxiety about anything, but in every circumstance and in everything, by prayer and petition (definite requests), with thanksgiving, continue to make your wants known to God. And God's peace (shall be yours, that tranquil state of a soul assured of its salvation through Christ, and so fearing nothing from God and being content with its earthly lot of whatever sort that is, that peace) which transcends all understanding shall garrison and mount guard over your hearts and minds in Christ Jesus (Philippians 4:6-7).

...neither are your ways My ways, says the Lord (Isaiah 55:8).

It had finally happened. I was on my way to the city where the Lord was leading me. The ministry position was secure, and my ministry associates had informed me that everything was working out for a job there in retail for me. In fact I was told that a job would be opening up about the time I got there, so needless to say, I was very excited. The

Words that the Lord had spoken to me during my times with Him were coming around perfectly. As I saw things opening up, my confidence level in the Lord's ways began to strengthen as well as my trust level. It is never easy believing God at face value. However, if we are to follow Him, we have to believe Him at His Word.

> *And so it was that he (Abraham), having waited long and endured patiently, realized and obtained (in the birth of Isaac as a pledge of what was to come) what God had promised him. Men indeed swear by a greater (than themselves), and with them in all disputes the oath taken for confirmation is final (ending strife). Accordingly God also, in His desire to show more convincingly and beyond doubt to those who were to inherit the promise the unchangeableness of His purpose and plan, intervened (mediated) with an oath. This was so that, by two unchangeable things (His promise and His oath) in which it is impossible for God ever to prove false or deceive us, we who have fled (to Him) for refuge might have mighty indwelling strength and strong encouragement to grasp and hold fast the hope appointed for us and set before (us)* (Hebrews 6:15-18).

God will never dishonor His Word. We must study it—not so much to memorize the Scripture—this will come to us on its own as we study. We are meditating upon God's Word so that we can have success in what we do, as He gives us instructions out of His Word by His Spirit. As God speaks His Word to our hearts, it comes alive within us. So rather than trying to keep instructions or become obedient to the law oriented, we are led along by the Holy Spirit, who brings life to the Scriptures. This is something that may seem hard to understand by reading it here; however, as we practice this kind of studying, we will better understand how God leads us and how His Word comes alive in us as we obey.

As we become more intimate with our heavenly Father, we will hear Him as a Person and not as a memory verse in our minds. God is quite capable of presenting and representing Himself, as I have shared in the writing of this book thus far. And of course, we see this very vividly in the Scriptures. God is not hiding. He wants to reveal Himself, but we must be willing to follow Him and be led by Him on His terms. If we allow Him to lead, then He will, without question, let us know that He is the One leading. He has ways of revealing Himself as we cooperate with Him that say very clearly, "This had to be God!"

Study and be eager and do your utmost to present yourself to God approved (tested by trial), a workman who has no cause to be ashamed, correctly analyzing and accurately dividing (rightly handling and skillfully teaching) the Word of Truth (2 Timothy 2:15).

But be doers of the Word (obey the message), and not merely listeners to it... (James 1:22).

For the Word that God speaks is alive and full of power (making it active, operative, energizing, and effective)... (Hebrews 4:12).

But solid food is for full-grown men, for those whose senses and mental faculties are trained by practice to discriminate and distinguish between what is morally good and noble and what is evil and contrary either to divine or human law (Hebrews 5:14).

Now it is easy to simply quote passages like these, but if we are to follow the Lord, we must allow these Words of His to penetrate deep within us—into our inner most being. As this happens, we will be able to distinguish God's voice and thoughts above our own. We will even begin to know when our heavenly Father is reasoning with us, bringing about clarity in our lives and revealing to us what we should do with His help. As this happens, intimacy is not a problem. When we experience for ourselves the love of God through His leading us, we begin to see that God is for us and not against us. This is how love grows beyond the salvation experience of accepting Jesus Christ as our Savior—we follow Him. Studying comes first—getting to know God better through the Scriptures, listening to Him in prayer, asking questions, believing Him for answers, then allowing Him to answer in ways that confirm "I Am the Lord." This is exciting, but it is also challenging, engaging us in a relationship with Christ that our heavenly Father intended us to have.

When I got into town, I drove to the Mall where I was told to go. I was to speak with a man there who was hiring. I was nervous. I was excited, but I was also wondering, still, how all this could be happening. I felt peace. I felt assurance. I believed that God was with me. As I walked through the Mall, the thought of being in a clothing store, selling clothes almost overwhelmed me. This had been a very strong desire in my heart for a long time, and now the Lord was bringing this about in reality.

When I saw the store I was very impressed with the way

that it looked. The man that I was supposed to see came right out and I told him who I was. It was then that I was shocked to hear what he had to say.

"We do not have any jobs available right now," he said. My stomach dropped. What hope I once had seemed to drop deep inside. It seemed as if his words repeated themselves over and over in my mind. He explained that he knew that I was coming into town, but there wasn't any work available at the time. Something might be coming up, he said. So I filled out an application. When he said that something might be coming up, it offered me some hope.

After I'd completed the application, I gave it to him and left the store. As I walked back to the parking lot, I did not know what I felt. I was hurt, yes; I was angry, yes. I was upset deeply and felt as if I had been lied to. Then the thoughts began to race in my mind about what could have been done differently, like, why didn't I wait until I heard back from my friends concerning the confirmation of the job. But then I thought, they had already felt that it was. How could this have happened? Suddenly I felt weak. I couldn't think. There I was, my car completely filled with everything I owned.

"Lord," I said, shaking, not really knowing what to say to Him. "What is this? Why has this happened? Why did You do this to me?" I felt abandoned. What do I do now? I leaned against my car and tried to calm myself. I knew in my heart of hearts that I had heard from God. I knew it, but I could not prove it. All I knew was that I had just been told that there was no job available, and I did not know when one would be. I had very little money to spend, and if I did not get a job soon, I would have to go back home. Imagine the shame I would have. Imagine all the questions people would have, and even if they did not ask questions, they would think that I was crazy. How could God have done this to me? I was in a position now of totally trusting Him. But He had promised me a job. He had asked me what I wanted to do. He had told me what to say to my dad, and now here I was, feeling abandoned.

"Go downtown," I heard Him say. Now, I did remember His voice.

"Alright, Lord," I said, hope slowly returning.

I had been to this town once before so I had a pretty good idea of where things were. Although I could not give directions by road names, I certainly knew where downtown was because the person that I would be living with for a while worked downtown. Surely, he would be able to help.

It did not take long to get downtown from the Mall. The city was small but growing. I found a parking space and went to the store where my ministry associate worked, and luckily, he was there. I tried to get past the greetings very quickly, because I was still upset about the job situation, and telling him about it was hard. He assured me that everything would work out and that the Lord would help. This was very reassuring as I looked in my car, seeing all that I owned. Then he told me to go up the street to a nearby clothing store because it might be interesting to look into. He told me that he knew the guy who managed it.

When I arrived at the store, I had a good feeling about it. Just the smell in the air—what I will call "retail" was encouraging. The guy who managed the store came out and introduced himself to me, and I began telling him who I was and about our mutual friend who worked at the other downtown store. Right away the gentleman recognized me, saying, "I've heard you sing before." That was a relief, and it caused me to relax.

"Oh, really. Where?" I asked, and he told me. This led

into a very good conversation, but then he also told me that there was not a job available. One of his workers had been in an accident and would be returning soon. Disappointed again.

"But if something comes up..." he said. Then I told him about how I had applied at the Mall and that the store was a sister store to his. It had been through his acquaintance with my future room mate that he knew I needed a job.

From there all I could do was drive out to the place where I would be living. I was deeply troubled and probably would have cried if I had been able to. I was hurt but I still felt a silent hope inside. It did not seem fair. *Had the Lord deceived me*, I thought. *How could this have happened?* In spite of the feelings I had, there was peace inside. Although it wasn't overwhelming at the time, it quieted all the other thoughts that were trying to bombard my heart.

It had been some weeks that I had been without a job, applying for some as I was given leads, but nothing happened. Then one day while I was sitting in the house, the Lord spoke to me.

"Do not apply for any other jobs." Not twenty minutes afterwards, the phone rang and it was the first gentleman whom I'd met at the Mall. He told me that he had contacted a former boss where I'd worked before, and that he wanted to hire me. I would be working at the downtown store and not the Mall. I thanked him and hung up the phone.

"Thank you, Father," I said. "Thank you!" I felt weakened physically by the way this had happened. God kept His Word to me. Now, it did not happen the way that I wanted it to or expected it to happen, but it did happen. God had set everything up beforehand, and He knew that my not being able to get a job right away would be a serious test for me; however, I passed the test by remaining in the city, believing that the Lord had sent me there.

Lean on, trust in, and be confident in the Lord with all your heart and mind and do not rely on your own insight or understanding. In all your ways know recognize, and acknowledge Him, and He will direct and make straight and plain your paths. Be not wise in your own eyes; reverently fear and worship the Lord and turn (entirely) away from evil (Proverbs 3:5-7).

Chapter 15

Good Thoughts About You

For the rest, brethren, whatever is true, whatever is worthy of reverence and is honorable and seemly, whatever is just, whatever is pure, whatever is lovely and lovable, whatever is kind and winsome and gracious, if there is any virtue and excellence, if there is anything worthy of praise, think on and weigh and take account of these things (fix your minds on them). Practice what you have learned and received and heard and seen in me, and model your way of living on it, and the God of peace (of untroubled, undisturbed well-being) will be with you (Philippians 4:8-9).

The way we think plays a very large part in the way that we perceive God. If we perceive Him as hard to please, distant, domineering, harsh, or that He will not give love to us until we prove that we are worthy of love, then intimacy with Him will be impossible. We grow to know that God wants to be involved in our lives by the way He responds to us and how He reveals Himself. We must learn to practice, asking God to show us Himself today. Our Christianity must

97

be relevant and relative to the times we live in. We must be able to see Christ operating and being active in our lives today. He does this through showing us that what concerns us concerns Him as well. Remember, however, that we must allow God to put forth His terms so that we get to know Him according to His way of revealing Himself and not how we perceive Him. God leaves an internal mark on our hearts so that His communication with us leaves deep and convincing evidence that we are getting to know Him.

And I will give them one heart (a new heart) and I will put a new spirit within them; and I will take the stony (unnaturally hardened) heart out of their flesh, and will give them a heart of flesh (sensitive and responsive to the touch of their God), that they may walk in My statutes and keep My ordinances, and do them... (Ezekiel 11:19-20).

As our hearts become sensitive and tender toward God, regarding Him as good to us, then we will begin to experience innocence. Innocence is that which causes us to believe God—regardless of what He tells us. And He will share things with us as we grow to know Him that He cannot in the earlier stages of our relationship with Him. He wants to talk to us about what troubles us, what makes us happy, why certain things happen, and often offering answers that we would not come up with on our own. And with God's answers and personal responses comes understanding—a settling within our hearts that settles issues even though we may not have the visible evidence that everything will be fine. But the one who continues to pursue Christ will find out how He lived in such peace on this earth with His Father.

So we must believe that God is good. We must approach Him this way, although everything that is happening in our lives may speak otherwise. But we do not measure God's goodness by what is happening around us, but according to what He is doing in us that affects us outwardly. This is important. "We love Him, because He first loved us" (1 John 4:19).

We press toward being open and honest with God about our feelings and what is important to us, because the more we talk with Him, the more we learn how to communicate with Him. We learn to communicate with Him because we learn to hear His voice, and in hearing His voice properly, we respond correctly. This causes us to be able to know His heart better for us. And in this kind of relationship—God speaking to us and our responding to Him—we begin to know Him and His love for us. God loves us deeply. His love is transforming. It even changes our minds about ourselves. And as our minds are being transformed, we can better know what God's desires are for us. And if we know what God's desires and plans for us are, then we are better able to walk them out in this life with His help.

> *Do not be conformed to this world (this age), (fashioned after and adapted to its external, superficial customs), but be transformed (changed) by the (entire) renewal of your mind (by its new ideals and its new attitude), so that you may prove (for yourselves) what is good and acceptable and perfect will of God, even the thing which is good and acceptable and perfect (in His sight for you)* (Romans 12:2).

Sensitivity develops as we open our hearts to God more.

Many times He will touch our hearts through recurring thoughts, things that may bother us, or things that we need to know about ourselves as well as Himself. God is a Father who sincerely cares about His children; however, we must be attentive to this truth and take advantage of it. This truth is available for us, and our heavenly Father is willing to share it freely, so that we know Him intimately. Let us remember that intimacy is something that is developed through trust. And if the ones we are to be intimate with are open and honest with us, this assists the relationship along—causing us to become more deeply involved with the welfare of each other.

What is important to you? What causes you to think more than anything else? Is it a special need? A relationship with Mom and Dad? That you go to school—perhaps finish school? We must consider that all these things are important to God. Remember, now, when you approach God, talk honestly with Him about what you feel. He is after that sensitive place within us that we often hide from Him, sometimes afraid that we cannot share what we feel so sensitively, as most of us have been hurt before. But we need to hear God's voice—and His voice represents accurately what is in His heart. Know for sure that God will never mislead you in any way.

Some years ago I began to feel really lonely. At first I could very easily drown the feelings by spending time with the Lord or doing things that kept me busy. Somehow in spite of my activity, the feeling would not go away. But I was beginning to trust the Lord more and more and knew that I could talk to Him about what I felt. So I drove to a park not too far from where I lived. I went there a lot because I enjoyed the water flowing from the dam as well as the natural beauty and quiet that being at the park afforded me.

It was close to dark when I went to the park that evening because I felt such a need to talk to the Lord about what I was feeling. I remember getting to the park and sitting there in the car. After awhile I began to notice couples walking on the sidewalk, holding hands, laughing and enjoying themselves. As I watched them, it occurred to me that something was wrong inside. At first, I did not want to admit it.

"What is wrong with me, Lord?" I asked.

"You are lonely," He said right away.

"Lonely?" I asked. I did not understand why I felt so lonely because I had such good company with the Lord, but I was lonely.

"It is not good for you to be alone," He said, causing me to remember what He had spoken about Adam. "You are not alone," He said to me. "But you are lonely. Would you like for me to give you a wife?" I was surprised at the thought and even honored. Just the thought of being married took me far away in my thoughts, and imagining it was pleasant for the moment.

"But I have you," I said to the Lord, somehow thinking that if I got married that I would be trading the Lord for a wife. It did not seem right.

"I know that you have Me," He said calmly. "And you always will; however, you are still lonely. If you will ask Me, I will give you a wife after My own heart." I looked up, having lowered my head to think for just a moment. There was yet another couple walking past as I looked up.

"Can I think about it?" I asked, still thinking of how much I loved Him. And at that time I did not want anything to compete with what I had with Him. You see, the Lord had actually become my first love, and I was really beginning to know what love was like in my time with Him. But He was considerate enough to bless me with whatever I needed.

"You may think about it," He said. "There is time. You wanted to know what was wrong with you, so I told you."

Now the Lord God said, It is not good (sufficient, satisfactory) that the man should be alone; I will make him a helper meet (suitable, adapted, complementary) for him (Genesis 2:18).

There are feelings that the Lord gives us—emotions that will sometime demand attention. And there is nothing wrong with these emotions; however, as we grow to know our heavenly Father's love and concern for us, we will also be able to naturally let Him know what we feel. He in turn will be able to speak to us, giving us the ability to know what we did not know and possibly could not know on our own.

Remember to think the right thoughts about God. Believe with all of your heart that He loves you and wants you with Him. He wants to speak with you often, revealing to you what you do not know, and better help you to understand what you do know.

Yes, marriage is important. It is a very significant event in our lives, and how wonderful it is to know that Jesus Christ so wants to be intimately involved with us to let us know that we need wives and husbands.

"I will give you some time to think about being married," the Lord told me. "If you change your mind, let Me know."

Chapter 16

There Is a Season

To everything there is a season, and a time for every matter or purpose under heaven: A time to be born and a time to die...(Ecclesiastes 3:1-2).

I have mentioned that God is concerned about whatever concerns us. But it is not easy to know this unless we spend time with Him on a regular basis to find out just how concerned He is about our natural lives. If we are honest with ourselves we will say that our primary focus in this world remains on our needs being met. The Father knows our needs before we even make them known to Him; however, it is an exciting thing when we engage in prayer with Him to watch how He brings about certain things.

Delight yourself also in the Lord, and He will give you the desires and secret petitions of your heart. Commit your way to the Lord (roll and repose each care of your load on Him); trust (lean on, rely on, and be confident) also in Him and He will bring it to pass (Psalm 37:4-5).

Meditating on God's words, particularly those things that He speaks to us personally, will enable us to recognize when He is speaking to us—either giving more insight into what He has already spoken or bringing other things into light. Either way, we must understand that our heavenly Father is a communicator, and if we obey the promptings of His Spirit within us, we will understand the timing by which He works. Admittedly, sometimes we will not understand how the Lord works—but we must be willing to trust Him. Trusting God is something that comes with time and age. As we learn and accept the revelation that God knows everything and that He keeps our best interests in heart, we will be more willing to trust Him with each aspect of our lives. Now, with this said, we will sometimes find it hard to yield our will to Father. Yes, this is true. Because we do not know everything from His perspective, we will want to cling to where we are presently in our walk with Him. This is where we feel most secure. However, things happen in life that require us to do things that may seem to alter what Father is doing presently, even though we may be doing exactly what He has instructed us to do.

After I had settled into the city where the Lord sent me, I began to sense that He was trying to send me home again. I fought against this sensing for quite sometime, because it did not make sense for me to have just moved here to this city as the Lord had instructed me to do, and then return home. It simply defied logic. But I knew that something was wrong. I could feel this constant prodding inside that I needed to go home, but I did not know what to do.

Feeling this way about possibly returning home was very difficult for me. I was beginning to like this new place in the Lord, and my life was going well. How could the Lord now be asking me to go back home—or, at least, that was what I

felt. I was too afraid to ask Him if what I was feeling was actually His leading me to return home. I just did not want to
do it. How could He be doing this to me? To look at it
anyone would say that it was confusing. It seemed contradictory. Would God contradict Himself? This inner turmoil
continued to grow, even to the point where I was losing my
peace. Finally, I submitted to ask Father what was wrong in
prayer.

"I want you to return home," He said.

"But I just got here," I responded, not listening for further instruction. I did not handle hearing going back home
well. What would people think? My family, for instance?
They would think that I had failed and was returning home,
and that God had not told me to leave as I had reported. It
did not seem fair. I would have to leave my job, and no one
would understand why I was leaving after waiting to get established.

"No," I said to the Lord. I was not open to discuss it, although I knew that I was wrong in speaking to the Lord un-
kindly. After saying no to Him I felt as if I pulled myself out
of His presence. It seemed as if I walked away from Him,
and that His influence over me was at a distance. After not
going to Him about the matter of going home again, I continued to feel more and more unhappy, until the dreams
began.

I had been very restless. Although I could sleep, I was
not sleeping the way that I would have liked to. I increas-
ingly tossed and turned until I'd fall asleep. But one night I
had this dream. In the dream, I saw a casket in the front of a
church. I could tell that the casket was open for viewing, but
no one was viewing the body that was in the casket. I remained at a distance so that I could not see the person inside. The image haunted me all the next day. Who could it

have been in the casket? The very next night I had the same dream, only this time I was closer to the casket than before, but still I refused to look inside it. I was afraid to—suppose it was me or someone that I knew. I struggled in my sleep until I awoke.

Finally, the third time I had the dream I was still standing at a distance, refusing to look, but I felt my resistance weakening. Then I looked and saw the Lord standing next to the head of the casket.

"Larry," He said. "If you will look and see who is in the casket, you will not have this dream again." Slowly I walked toward the opened casket and looked inside. As I looked down at the face in it, I saw my dad. At first I felt shock. I could not believe that it was my father lying in the casket. Then suddenly I felt love and peace as I stood there before the casket along with the Lord, Who stood just at the front of it. As I took a longer look at Dad in the casket, the Lord closed the cover slowly, until I could not see Daddy's face any longer. I knew then that my dad was going to pass away, and that was what the Lord had been trying to tell me.

"Larry, your father has been sick for some time," He later explained, when I was willing to listen and not fight His sending me back home. "That is why I want you to return home. Your brother has been taking care of him, but you need to go home now and take care of him."

Not long after the Lord had told me these things, I spoke to my oldest brother and he told me how sick our dad was. I was surprised as no one had told me to the degree that he had been sick, and now it was time for me to leave this city and go home to see about my Dad. But there was one thing that began to bother me about all that was going on. Where was my dad in his relationship with God? Although my dad was a very good man, I did not know whether or not he had accepted Jesus Christ as His Savior. This caused me great concern, and I knew that this issue had to be settled in my heart before he went on to be with the Lord.

Chapter 17

He Will Be With You

Because he has set his love upon Me, therefore will I deliver him. I will set him on high, because he knows and understands My name (has a personal knowledge of My mercy, love, and kindness—trusts and relies on Me, knowing I will never forsake him, no never). He shall call upon Me, and I will answer him, I will be with him in trouble, I will deliver him and honor him. With long life will I satisfy him and show him My salvation (Psalm 91:14).

Bear in mind that God knows everything. He knows everything all at once, and in this knowledge of His, He reveals to us what we need to know.

Let be and be still, and know (recognize and understand) that I am God... (Psalm 46:10).

If we are to hear from God and to know Him more intimately, then we must be willing to have our lives adjusted to His way of doing things. God wants us to have wonderful lives, and we can, if we listen to Him. There are many things that could be avoided in our lives if we listen to God and honor His wisdom, counsel, and instruction. We cannot avoid all things that happen, but if we live by faith, then our faith in God gives us strength in any given situation. However, we must hear from God on a regular basis and allow Him to influence us. This can be done without us becoming introverted and not having anything to do with others. I have seen that the more I fellowship with our heavenly Father, the more able I am to enjoy the company of others. Being with and getting to know God increases our security in who we are. This happens because the more we know about our heavenly Father, the more we learn about ourselves. Obedience is the key in growing to know God more intimately. As we obey the Lord we will understand Him better. This understanding includes an acceptance of His ways, desiring them above our own. I do want to point out that we will always have our own will—presenting us with the ability to obey or disobey our heavenly Father. However, once we are trained to obey the Lord, this yielding of the will becomes easier. It was not until I understood that my dad was sick that I was willing to listen to the Lord and go back home.

It was not as difficult as I thought it would be to return home. I appreciated the Lord showing me what was happening and giving me the opportunity to come home and be with my dad at this time in his life. Admittedly, I was concerned about having seen him in a casket. This vision haunted me for quite sometime. I did not know when or if this would happen, but I felt in my heart that whatever was going to happen would be happening soon.

When I did come home I found that my dad was sicker than I had realized. My brother had never given me a bad report, but I could tell that our dad was getting weaker and a lot less able to do what he had done before. At one time in his life, he had been a very strong man—a farmer—able to lift heavy loads, work from early in the morning to later in the day, but now he had diminished somewhat, spending a lot of time simply falling asleep while trying to get things done. This sight was sad but I maintained my composure, not at all sharing with him what I had dreamed. My dad realized that he needed me there. I told him that I would stay with him and take care of him, and he never argued. He seemed to have accepted the fact that he could not live by himself. Because of health issues, my mother was living with her sister and could not care properly for herself, so each of my parents required care from others.

I remember one evening when I came home from being with friends, I felt as if something was about to happen, but I did not know what. Since I had been home, everything seemed to have been alright with Dad and me. He was doing well, knowing that someone was there with him, which brought some consolation to me. I took him to the doctor regularly, as he was a kidney dialysis outpatient, requiring frequent help. We had begun enjoying our frequent 30 minute drives to the doctor. It seemed we were becoming more like friends rather than father and son. I rather liked this relationship with him; however, I needed to know that he was ready to go on and be with the Lord.

The thought of his passing was not tormenting because I had already accepted it. The Lord had given me another dream about my father. In this dream I saw the dogwood trees blooming. They were absolutely beautiful. My dad and I walked together among the blooming dogwoods, and I said to him, "Aren't these trees beautiful?"

"Yes....they are...." he replied.

"He will pass away when the dogwoods begin to

bloom...." The Lord had told me. And it was almost spring time when the trees began to bloom.

This particular night when I drove home I had not had much peace when I was with my friends. We had prayed, and one of them in particular had felt that something grave was about to happen in my life, but he did not know what.

As I sat in the car alone that evening, entertaining mixed emotions, I started to open the door to get out of the car, when the Lord spoke to me.

"Sit here for a moment. I want to talk to you," He said.

"Larry," He began. "I brought you home so that you could be with your dad. Soon, he will be coming home to be with me. He will not die as men think of dying, but he will go to sleep. When he wakes up, he will be in My presence."

"So he is...." I began to say saved, but could not finish the sentence. The Lord stopped me.

"I have not forgotten the commitment that your father made with me many years ago. He belongs to Me." Hearing this, my heart was now relieved. "Larry, I knew that if your father's death caught you off guard that it would hurt you very much. That is why I wanted you to come home. You love Me very much, and I did not want this to harm you."

"Lord, do you know how much I love you?" I asked. "Do you really know how much I love you?"

"Yes," He said. "I know that you love Me more than food—more than anything, I know that you love Me. Do you know how much I love you?" He asked. Afterwards, I began to cry. I could feel such love coming from the Lord, and I knew that it would not be long before my dad passed away. My heart was now settled and I had peace about my dad's passing. What I did not know or possibly did not have the courage to speak about with my dad, the Lord had settled the issue.

My dad passed away early the next morning. It was the beginning of the spring, when the dogwood trees begin to bloom.

Intimacy with God is a powerful tool—it is a relationship that allows our heavenly Father to reveal His heart to us. Much like Abraham's relationship with God, He wants to let us know things that can potentially harm or be very painful to us. We can have this kind of relationship with Christ, if we allow ourselves to be still, pressing past what we think is important into what He esteems important.

> *And the Lord said, Shall I hide from Abraham (My friend and servant) what I am going to do...* (Genesis 18:17).

We must be willing to go past what we see with our eyes if we want to observe the actions of our heavenly Father. Remember that God knows everything, and if we are willing to have our minds stretched or renewed, then our heavenly Father can show us anything.

> *Since we consider and look not to the things that are seen but to the things that are unseen; for the things that are visible are temporal (brief and fleeting), but the things that are invisible are deathless and everlasting* (2 Corinthians 4:18).

Chapter 18

God's Friends

But you, Israel, My servant, Jacob, whom I have chosen, the offspring of Abraham My friend (Isaiah 41:8).

And (so) the Scripture was fulfilled that says, Abraham believed in (adhered to, trusted in, and relied on) God, and this was accounted to him as righteousness (as conformity to God's will in thought and deed), and he was called God's friend (Hebrews 2:23).

And he (Abraham) believed in (trusted in, relied on, remained steadfast to) the Lord, and He counted it to him as righteousness (right standing with God) (Genesis 15:6).

For the past few chapters I have shared much about how the Lord spoke to me, led me, as well as the results of being faithful to the Lord. However, in writing, it is difficult to share the difficulties that plagued my senses as I followed the Lord. It is important to know that once we determine to follow Christ, our lives will change totally. It is inevitable. God has plans that we cannot know by our senses. If we could, most of us would follow those plans; however, because God has set up the works that He wants us to do beforehand—before we ever existed—it is by His leading that we find and follow that path. And, as I said, it is not easy because the ways of God are not common to men. We do become familiar with the way that God does things as we yield ourselves to Him, but we will oftentimes find ourselves in conflicting or contradictory circumstances that say God has not spoken to us.

It is during these times that we must trust our experience with God. Although the method by which God does things changes and wavers, He does not change in His consistent nature. He is always honest, up front, truthful, and will never deceive us. It may seem as if there is no way that what we have heard from God will happen. This is simply how our Father has set it up. This is also how our faith takes us past what we see in the natural. Each time the Father spoke to me personally, the majority of the times nothing He said seemed possible or even probable. However, obedience to God's spoken words to me brought about the possibility of obedience. Now, many of us will hear God speak to us—but hearing alone is not enough. We must do what the Father tells us in order to see the validity behind what He says.

> *But be doers of the Word (obey the message), and not merely listeners to it, betraying yourselves (into deception by reasoning contrary to the Truth) (James 1:22).*

> *For indeed we have had the glad tidings (Gospel of*

God) proclaimed to us just as truly as they (the Israelites of old did when the good news of deliverance from bondage came to them); but the message they heard did not benefit them, because it was not mixed with faith (with the leaning of the entire personality on God in absolute trust and confidence in His power, wisdom, and goodness) by those who heard it... (Hebrews 4:2).

But the natural, nonspiritual man does not accept or welcome or admit into his heart the gifts and teachings and revelations of the Spirit of God, for they are folly (meaningless nonsense) to him; and he is incapable of knowing them (of progressively recognizing, understanding, and becoming better acquainted with them) because they are spiritually discerned and estimated and appreciated (1 Corinthians 2:14).

We must keep an open mind when we come into our Father's presence, seeking Him for counsel or direction. Our Father wants to give us such direction and counsel; however, it may not always appeal to us or be on the terms we expect. Primarily, when it comes to direction, the Lord wants us to fully trust Him. This is how we become our heavenly Father's friends. We accept what our Father tells us, believe it, whether or not we understand it, and follow through His plans as He leads us. Eventually, as we continue to yield ourselves to our Father's voice and Spirit, we will know exactly that He is leading us. We will not have to hear a voice speaking to us—His presence within will be like a perfectly tuned compass, telling us that this is what we should do. Jesus said this: "You are My friends if you keep on doing the things which I command you to do" (John 15:14).

Simply to look at a passage such as this, we could wonder: "How could Jesus possibly expect us to trust Him at face value?" We must understand that Jesus had walked with His disciples for sometime, showing them the ways of the Father, giving them time to ask questions, and to see the salvation of God working through Him for them as well as those whom they encountered. In order for us to better engage in and understand being friends with God, we must believe that God wants to begin a deep, sensitive and intimate relationship with us. He wants to take away the distance that we often have felt even as we have been Christians for quite sometime. Yes, it is possible for us to be able to hear God speak about future events, to calm us, to warn us of impending danger, and to let us know about our loved ones; however, the question that is put before us: "Do we believe that God is able to do this?"

Unless we are willing to simply believe that our sins have been completely washed away by the blood of Jesus and that our heavenly Father does not see us as sinners, it will be difficult to embrace this kind of relationship. None of us are capable of walking perfectly in our flesh before God. We will sin occasionally, but there is a difference between occasional failure and consistent disobedience. The one who continues in Christ Jesus will see such an intimate relationship with Jesus possible.

By this we shall come to know (perceive, recognize, and understand) that we are of the Truth, and can reassure (quiet, conciliate, and pacify) our hearts in His presence. Whenever our hearts in (tormenting) self-accusation make us feel guilty and

condemn us. (For we are in God's hands), and He
knows (perceives and understands) everything
(nothing is hidden from Him) (1 John 3:19-20).

We must always remember that God is the God of faith.
We cannot please Him without active faith in our lives. The
testimonies that I have shared in this writing rest upon the
faithfulness of God. He is the One who initiated our relationship. He caused me, through revealing His apparent
love, to feel welcome to come into His presence often. And
the more that I have come into His presence, closely fellow-
shipping with Him, I have felt secure. Not only have I felt secure in Him, I have grown to trust Him, no matter what He
tells me. Whenever we begin to trust our heavenly Father, it
opens the door for more of His wisdom to flood our hearts.
We are able to better see and accept the revelation that
comes from Him as we simply believe. The actual process of
waiting on God to produce what He speaks is a process;
however, as we trust Him, He supports us during those
times.

That (Spirit) is the guarantee of our inheritance
(the first fruits, the pledge and foretaste, the down
payment on our heritage), in anticipation of its full
redemption and our acquiring (complete) posses-
sion of it—to the praise of His glory. For this reason,
because I have heard of your faith in the Lord Jesus
and your love toward all the saints (the people of
God). I do not cease to give thanks for you, making
mention of you in my prayers. (For I always pray
to) the God of our Lord Jesus Christ, the Father of
glory, that He may grant you a spirit of wisdom and
revelation (of insight into mysteries and secrets) in

the (deep and intimate) knowledge of Him. By having the eyes of your heart flooded with light, so that you can know and understand the hope to which He has called you, and how rich is His glorious inheritance in the saints (His set-apart ones) (Ephesians 1:14-18).

(Remember) that you were at that time separated (living apart) from Christ (excluded from all part in Him), utterly estranged and outlawed from the rights of Israel as a nation, and strangers with no share in the sacred compacts of the (Messianic) promise (with no knowledge of or right in God's agreements, His covenants). And you had no hope (no promise), you were in the world without God, but now in Christ Jesus, you who were (so) far away, through (by, in) the blood of Christ have been brought near (Ephesians 2:12-13).

Many times we struggle to believe that we are seated with Christ our Savior because we believe less about ourselves than we ought to. But Christ has afforded us seating with Him and our heavenly Father through His blood—not through works of our own. The work has been completed in Christ Jesus, so we now have peace with God.

By abolishing in His (own crucified) flesh the enmity (caused by) the Law with its decrees and ordinances (which He annulled); that He from the two might create in Himself one new man (one new quality of humanity out of the two), so making peace...And He came and preached the glad tidings of peace to you who were afar off and (peace) to those who were near. For it is through Him that we both (whether far off or near) now have an introduction (access) by one (Holy) Spirit to the Father (so that we are able to approach Him) (Ephesians 2:15,17-18).

As we continue to be mindful of this great sacrifice of Jesus Christ and listen for the voice of His Spirit within us, believing Him will become second nature to us. And as we listen to His voice, learning it in an intimate way, we will begin to see how excellently we can be led along by Him. First, however, we must fully believe that Christ will speak to us as friends—not slaves or those who barely made it into His kingdom—but those for whom He died, enabling us to enjoy fellowship with Him as our Father and Friend.

Chapter 19

God Shows His Love

In this the love of God was made manifest (displayed) where we are concerned; in that God sent His Son, the only begotten or unique (Son), into the world so that we might live through Him. In this is love; not that we loved God, but that He loved us and sent His Son to be the propitiation (the atoning sacrifice) for our sins. Beloved, if God loved us so (very much), we also ought to love one another (1 John 4:9-10).

What we were taught about God in our earlier years by our parents or others tends to remain our view of Him. For this reason, we often hear people ask, "Why did God do this or why did God allow this to happen?" not understanding that God had no part in whatever took place. It is essential that if we are going to walk with God, then we must understand the way He does things.

We can better understand God, but must be careful not to put Him in a box. As we better acquaint ourselves with Him and He reveals Himself to us more, we begin to see God as He really is. If we do not know that God is kind, then we will perceive Him as hard and harsh. If we do not know that God is merciful, then we will have trouble believing that He readily forgives us when we ask Him to.

I am writing to you, fathers, because you have come to know (recognize, be aware of, and understand) Him Who (has existed) from the beginning (1 John 2:13).

This passage suggests maturity. Fathers are those who have come to know God more intimately. What they have learned about Christ experientially, they are able to pass on to others, thus making even the children to be mature in their knowledge of Christ. We begin somewhere with Christ. We are not born as adults and neither are we born again knowing everything about Christ. We have the potential by the Holy Spirit's indwelling power to know all that Christ affords us. If we are to grow consistently, then we must remain steadfast in our desire to know Christ intimately.

(We are writing) about the Word of Life (in) Him Who existed from the beginning, Whom we have heard, Whom we have seen with our (own) eyes, Whom we have gazed upon (for ourselves) and have touched with our (own) hands. And the Life (an aspect of His being) was revealed (made manifest, demonstrated), and we saw (as eye witnesses) and are testifying to and declare to you the Life, the eternal Life (in Him) Who already existed with the Father and Who (actually) was made visible (was revealed) to us (His followers). What we have seen and (ourselves) heard, we are also telling you, so that you too may realize and enjoy fellowship as

*partners and partakers with us. And (this) fellow-
ship that we have (which is a distinguishing mark
of Christians) is with the Father and with His Son
Jesus Christ (the Messiah)* (1 John 1:1-3).

*One of His disciples, whom Jesus loved (whom He
esteemed and delighted in), was reclining (next to
Him) on Jesus' bosom* (John 13:23).

John had a very intimate relationship with Jesus. He
knew the heart of Jesus and remained with Him throughout
the most difficult of times. John primarily wrote of the love
of Christ, and this deep understanding of the love of God
permeated their relationship. John must have been able to
penetrate the heart of Jesus through sincere trust. We know
that Jesus loved all His disciples, but we must also believe
that for those who press more deeply to know God, the
depth of His love is revealed to them.

*Then you will seek Me, inquire for, and require Me
(as a vital necessity) and find Me when you search
for Me with all your heart* (Jeremiah 29:13).

We cannot seek God without being influenced by His
love. God reveals Himself and in this revelation we see His
love. If we are not careful, oftentimes this revelation of God
will cause us to feel inadequate. As God reveals His glory, we
feel inadequate and insufficient, but we must remember that
we are now able to approach God through the blood sacrifice of Jesus Christ. Knowing this truth affords us the confidence we have lacked in our approach to know God more
intimately. Confidence allows us to approach God without
fear—knowing that He welcomes us and that He wants us in

His Presence. It also gives us the ability to pray with confidence and accuracy.

> *And this is the confidence (the assurance, the privilege of boldness) which we have in Him; (we are sure) that if we ask anything (make any request) according to His will (in agreement with His own plan), He listens to and hears us. And if (since) we (positively) know that He listens to us in whatever we ask, we also know (with settled and absolute knowledge) that we have (granted us as our present possessions) the requests made of Him* (1 John 5:14-15).

We must understand that this privilege of boldness increases—not in the form of arrogance or pride in the fact that we know God—and genuine humility is more deeply defined in our hearts.

It is important that we do not forget that we are human beings in our approach to God. We must also remember that we cannot bypass Christ's humanity and get to His deity. If we remain just as we are—human beings in our approach to God—then we will better understand how Jesus was able to live as a human being among us. Part of Jesus' human experience was that He saw people's needs and had the ability to assess as well as apply what was needed to help them. As we follow Jesus' example, we will know how to relate to our heavenly Father—not so much in the miracles He performed, but in His personal relationship with His heavenly Father. Understanding this relationship will better help us to comprehend how Jesus became the Savior of mankind.

In the days of His flesh (Jesus) offered up definite,

special petitions (for that which He not only wanted but needed) and supplications with strong crying and tears to Him Who was (always) able to save Him (out) from death, and He was heard because of His reverence toward God (His godly fear, His piety, in that He shrank from the horrors of separation from the bright presence of the Father). Although He was a Son, He learned (active, special) obedience through what He suffered, and (His completed experience) making Him perfectly (equipped), He became the Author and Source of eternal salvation to all those who give heed and obey Him (Hebrews 5:7-9).

Therefore He is able also to save to the uttermost (completely, perfectly, finally, and for all time and eternity) those who come to God through Him, since He is always living to make petition to God and intercede with Him and intervene for them (Hebrews 7:25).

Embracing Christ's Humanity

Because we have been born of God's Spirit, the truth that we see in Hebrews 7:25 becomes a part of us as we engage in everyday activity with the Lord Jesus, participating with Him in what we might consider unimportant things. The way that we get to know Jesus more intimately is by including Him, asking Him questions, and allowing Him to reveal Himself in the same way that He lived as a human being in the earth. As we do this, Jesus will be able to reveal Himself to us as a supernatural Savior or in more profound ways. By embracing His humanity, it will be a lot easier to understand His deity. Although we are not deity, we are sons of the Most High God, and we possess the life of God within.

Because the Holy Spirit has given us this life, we can closely associate with Christ—even in His suffering; however, we are not to remain in consistent suffering, but are to engage in resurrection power as well.

The Spirit Himself (thus) testifies together with our own spirit, (assuring us) that we are children of God. And if we are (His) children, then we are (His) heirs also; heirs of God and fellow heirs with Christ (sharing His inheritance with Him); only we must share His suffering if we are to share His glory (Romans 8:16-17).

Now as we grow together in love with Jesus Christ, we begin to understand Him and see Him more clearly—but we need to embrace His humanity first and embrace the cross of Christ as our means of total salvation. Once we embrace this to the point that our hearts fully accept it, Christ is further and more deeply revealed to us. He is then able to show us things about others.

Christ is about reaching out to others. Once we are secure in Him ourselves, He reveals to us the needs and cares of others. Jesus takes a personal interest in what we are going through because it usually leads us to Him. And if we allow His intervention, He is able to show Himself to us, causing us to see how much He loves us. And as varying as life itself, so the love of Christ is revealed to, for, and through us.

In the closing chapters of this book I want to share how powerful the love of God is for others, and how He leads us, if we will allow Him.

Chapter 20

When Things Are Wrong

When we accept Jesus Christ as our Savior and begin to learn about Him in practical ways, we also become more sensitive to His presence. We begin to become very aware that Jesus Christ was indeed a real Person with real feelings. If we understand this better, then it should not come as a surprise when we begin to be more sensitive to the things that affect our friends, family, co-workers, or acquaintances. Jesus was a caring Person, and if we are to walk with Him more intimately, then we must be ready to feel what He felt for people.

I know that saying this might cause some to be alarmed; however, we must understand that if we continue to keep our lives open for the Holy Spirit's influence, then we must also be ready for Him to fulfill God's purposes in our lives. I want to share a certain experience that happened some years ago when I was much younger in the Lord.

I remember going to work one day at a local grocery store, where I worked as a bagger. I won friends very easily and for some reason, I was particularly influential in the lives of those who were much younger than I was. I cannot explain it, but I had certain sensitivity for what teenagers were going through. On this particular day, a friend of mine, whom I will call David, was having what appeared to be a bad day. I felt it more than I could see it in his actions, and was troubled by it. I also found that in trying to communicate with him, he was short with me in conversation and would get up and leave before I could talk at length about what might be troubling him. This bothered me because he was normally not like this. I know that we can say things to irritate others and can do things that might cause them not to want to be around us, but this had a different feel about it. After I had sorted though my own mind what might be wrong, I came to the conclusion that something was wrong that I could not quite understand, and David was not being very helpful.

During a break at work, we ended up in the break room at the same time, so I tried to take advantage of the few minutes we had together to speak with him.

"What's wrong?" I asked. I could tell that he was dispirited. It was all over his face. Normally David was upbeat, and I had never seen him like this before. Granted, teenagers have their problems, but this was much unlike him. What could I do to help him?

"Nothing," he said, rather abruptly, indicating that he did not care to talk about anything. Perhaps it was girl trouble.

"Are you sure?" I asked.

"Well..." I remember him looking at me with sorrow and even confusion in his eyes, but he would not betray what was bothering him.

"David, there is something wrong, and I want to help you."

"I want to tell you, but I can't," he said. It seemed as if there was something he needed to say, but he wouldn't. I was hoping that he would let me know what was wrong, as I felt that something terrible was about to happen. It was a feeling that I cannot describe. Inside, the Holy Spirit was practically kicking me to get David to talk to me.

"Is it that bad?" I asked, moments later.

He responded only with a sigh.

"David...."

"I can't tell you," he said, then stormed out of the break room. After that I did not have another opportunity to speak with him, but during the entire work shift I felt very concerned about him. The best way that I can describe it was like having an inner certainty that something was wrong and something bad could happen as a result if nothing was done. But the Holy Spirit did not show me anything about the situation troubling David. I just thought to myself that it would be okay. David would get over whatever it was that was bothering him in time.

The next day at work I found out that something terrible had happened. Our supervisor and others were talking about what had happened to David the night before. He had driven to the lake and killed himself in his car by carbon monoxide poisoning. The news shocked me. Obviously I thought, *Why couldn't I have done anything?* and *How could this have happened to someone so close to me?* but no clarity came concerning David. Why had I not been able to hear from God about such an occurrence and then do something about it? I would find out later.

Some days after David's death, I could not seem to get it out of my mind. I did not go to the funeral, but I was told that his father took his death very badly. I had heard that he was so grief stricken that he was carried outside of the church during the services. I did not feel guilty about not being able to help David since he had refused any help, but I wished that I could have done something.

After I heard the news about how his father was so grief stricken, it seemed that my feelings grew worse about not being able to help David. I felt compassion for his father, knowing that he must have been completely devastated by such an unexplained loss. Until this day, I do not know if anyone ever really knew why David did this to himself. But I do know that I had told him about the Lord on one or two occasions, and he listened. David was a good listener, and whenever he did talk to me at work, he knew that I listened to him and cared about what he had to say. I never tried to push my faith on him, but I did talk candidly about Jesus with him—making Jesus more real to him than what he had heard and seen on some occasions. Then one night I had a dream.

I do not have what can be called spiritual dreams often. The Holy Spirit speaks to me a lot during my quiet times with Him, but when I dream certain dreams, I know that they come from God. They leave me with the sense that I must do something or that something is going to happen that the Lord wants me to know about.

> *The (reverent) fear of the Lord is clean, enduring forever; the ordinances of the Lord are true and righteous altogether. More to be desired are they than gold, even than much fine gold; they are sweeter also than honey and drippings from the honeycomb. Moreover, by them is Your servant warned (reminded, illuminated, and instructed); and in keeping them there is great reward* (Psalm 119:10-11).

I do want to point out that the continued concern that I had for David still haunted me, but that did not cause the dream, I do not believe. In the dream I could clearly see a car and recognized it as being David's. The Lord allowed me to see David sitting behind the wheel of the car as it idled. He was not dead at the time, but I could see his mouth moving—he was praying. He was asking the Lord to save him, to forgive him. Even though the words were soft and hard to understand, I heard them. I then knew that he was alright with the Lord. After the dream, the Lord spoke to me, saying; "I want you to go and see his father. He is very concerned about his son, but I want him to know that his son is with Me. He is alright."

This brought much needed relief to me, and I knew it would relieve his father. As I mentioned earlier, I did not know David's father well. We had only been introduced in a brief conversation shortly before David's death.

As the days went by I did all the things I could to find David's father; however, I was not able to do so. I began to have times of doubt that I would find him, but the question remained in my mind: *Why would Father ask me to do something that I cannot do?* This kept the momentum going within me to find him.

God at Work

Sometimes in our efforts to please and obey God, we can forget that even in doing what the Father has called us to do, it is still His ability working within us to get His work done. Father wants us to enjoy and have fun in our working *with* Him, not so much working *for* Him. Our heavenly Father's heart is to do away with a works mentality. If we continue to feel that we have to work for God, then this attitude will also put within us the desire to get paid for our work. However, if we are working alongside Him—working with Him—then we understand that He repays us in full as we move along with Him. I am not speaking concerning financial gain, but every need is met as we allow Him to reveal Himself to us. Now, we must also understand that we are engaging in intimacy with Him—again, learning how to do what we see Him doing and to speak what we hear Him speaking, which becomes easier as we know Christ more fully. Intimacy cannot be substituted by doing things for God; however, through the things we do for God—engaging with Him in these efforts—we experience Him, and experiencing God at work with us helps us to know Him more personally.

One day, I became exasperated in my search to find David's father. I called a few people who might know him without any success. I tried going to one or two places where I had seen him before, but had no luck there either. No one knew where he could be found.

"Father, why did you tell me to find this man? I am clueless as to what to do." But I knew that I would find him one way or the other. The spoken words of God are words that bring life or come to pass at an appropriate time. When God speaks, His words come forth with authority. The words of Christ are meant to attach themselves and become an integral part of our being, for the words of Christ have creative power and lead us into the direction that God desires. God knew that when He told me to find David's father that I would be able to find him because I knew the Lord had told me to do so. And because Father's words were now a part of my life, burning within me, I would not stop searching until I found the man.

God watches over His word to perform it when it is the right time for it to be performed. When it comes to the way that God prepares people to hear from Him, I believe He prepares them in advance. So when they finally hear His words from someone whom God decides to send their way, they listen, even though they may not be what we would consider ready to accept them. Words are funny. Sometimes they have to be filtered through our consciousness, even more so when they are said to have come or be coming from God.

> *No one is able to come to Me unless the Father Who sent Me attracts and draws him and gives him the desire to come to Me, and (then) I will raise him up (from the dead) at the last day* (John 6:44).

We must understand that God is the One who must prepare the hearts of people for what He wants to say to them. Part of our sharing in the divine nature is being able to know the heart of our Father for one another—we must develop love for one another. This love that we should have for one another is not developed unless we are becoming more intimately acquainted with our heavenly Father. As we begin to understand the love that our heavenly Father has, not only for us individually but for others as well, we better understand how to share the words we believe are coming to them from the Lord.

One day I went to a local school to get some papers copied. I remember that as I was finishing up, the Holy Spirit spoke very clearly to me.

"You must hurry," He said. I did not question Him at this point, I moved ahead quickly to finish copying the papers. Once I was finished and went outside, the Holy Spirit's instructions continued. "When you turn out of the school parking lot, go right." At this point I was beginning to get very excited, anticipating something special was about to happen. I felt purpose in what I was hearing from the Lord,

and knew that I was actually being engaged with Him to accomplish something of significance. "When you get to the
stop sign up the road, turn to the left." Although I was very
familiar with this road, what was important was following
the instructions of the Holy Spirit. "Keep straight," He told
me after the turn. "Eventually, you know that this road ends
at an intersection and you must stop!"

When I got to the stop sign at the intersection, I saw a
truck passing by. Much to my surprise, it was David's father.
He did not see me, and it was good that no traffic was
coming and I was able to get out on the road right away and
drive up right beside him. I could not believe that this was
happening. Once I pulled up beside him, he saw and recognized me. It was then that I threw up my hand, waving at
him to pull over somewhere.

"I need to talk to you," I shouted. He nodded that he understood. Afterwards, I pulled in front of him and further
down the road I pulled into the parking lot of an old gym.
Finally, I was feeling some relief that I would be able to tell
him what the Lord had put in my heart. It was good that
David's father had understood that I needed to speak with
him, and he pulled into the parking lot directly behind me.
It took me a moment to compose myself, catching my
breath, and trying to accept and believe the Lord had led
me so perfectly.

"How are you?" I asked as we came face to face.

Trembling, he said, "Okay."

"I have something to tell you," I said. Then suddenly I
remembered how David had told him about me when we
were introduced. The Lord calmed me down and quietly
said, "He will believe you."

"The Lord showed me how hurt and sad you've been
since David's death, and He wanted me to tell you that

David is all right. Don't worry any more. Don't be sad any more," I told him.

When I said this, I could see the relief on his face as well as the surprise in his eyes.

"He knows that you are a man of God," the Lord reassured me, and I thanked the Lord for His emotional support.

When this time was over with David's father, I was able to finally rest. The Lord had done what He needed to get done through me. He had perfectly led me to David's father after having put it on my heart weeks before. Amazingly, David's father asked no questions. His words were very few, but he simply believed me. I am sure that once he had the time to think through what I had said, his heart became peaceful, and the Lord was able to do even a much deeper work in his life.

(Not in your own strength) for it is God Who is all the while effectually at work in you (energizing and creating in you the power and desire), both to will and to work for His good pleasure (Philippians 2:13).

The steps of a (good) man are directed and established by the Lord when He delights in his way (and He busies Himself with his every step). Though he falls, he shall not be utterly cast down, for the Lord grasps his hand in support and upholds him (Psalm 37:23-24).

Chapter 21

Better Faith

Now faith is the assurance (the confirmation, the title deed) of the things (we) hope for, being the proof of things (we) do not see and the conviction of their reality (faith perceiving as real fact what is not revealed to the senses). For by (faith—trust and holy fervor born of faith) the men of old had divine testimony borne to them and obtained a good report. By faith we understand that the worlds (during the successive ages) were framed (fashioned, put in order, and equipped for their intended purpose) by the word of God, so that what we see was not made out of things which are visible (Hebrews 11:1-3).

For in the Gospel a righteousness which God ascribes is revealed both springing from faith and leading to faith (disclosed through the way of faith that arouses to more faith). As it is written, The man who through faith is just and upright shall live and shall live by faith (Romans 1:18).

Sometimes we complicate faith. I believe this is because we do not understand faith as we should. Sometimes we look at the stories in the Bible about those who had great faith and we compare ourselves to them; however, we must keep a level head, realizing and knowing that these were people just like we are. They did not begin with the kind of faith that parted the Red Sea or closed the mouths of lions; they learned to trust and believe God by having intimate times of prayer with Him.

Now when Daniel knew that the writing was signed, he went into his house, and his windows being open in his chamber toward Jerusalem, he got down upon his knees three times a day and prayed and gave thanks before his God, as he had done previously (Daniel 6:10).

If we read the full story behind this passage of Scripture, we find that Daniel's enemies had hoped to trap him into being killed in the lions' den.

Then the presidents and satraps sought to find occasion (to bring accusation) against Daniel concerning the kingdom, but they could find no occasion or fault, for he was faithful, nor was there any error or fault found in him. Then said these men, We shall not find any occasion (to bring accusation) against this Daniel except we find it against him concerning the law of his God. Then these presidents and satraps came (tumultuously) together to the king and said to him, King Darius, live forever! All the presidents of the kingdom, the deputies and the satraps, the counselors and the governors, have

*consulted and agreed that the king should establish
a royal statute and make a firm decree that whoever shall ask a petition of any god or man for
thirty days, except of you, O king, shall be cast into
the den of lions...so King Darius signed the writing
and the decree* (Daniel 6:4-7,9).

Now, the question would be, why would Daniel continue
to pray to God when such a decree had been written and
signed by the king? We know that Daniel had great favor
with the king, as the Lord had previously used him to help
the king, and everything that Daniel did was successful. We
can only conclude that it was because Daniel had an excellent spirit toward God. How does one obtain or acquire this
excellence? It comes by the desire to obey the Lord and to
honor Him at His word. If we honor God, He will also honor
us.

In reading the book of Daniel, we can tell that Daniel
had a great love for God. We can also see that Daniel was
loved by God because of His desire for God and for the
people of God.

*And behold, a hand touched me, which set me (un-
steadily) upon my knees and upon the palms of my
hands. And (the angel) said to me, O Daniel, you
greatly beloved man...* (Daniel 10:10-11).

Daniel loved God, and we know that God loved Daniel.
God revealed the destiny of His people to Daniel. Now, we
can say that God had to use someone to reveal this great
revelation to, but He did not use just anyone. He revealed
Himself and His plans to someone who was genuinely
faithful and who loved and cared for Him. But Daniel grew

in his faith and love toward God. Daniel had seen God move on occasion and knew that He would help His people. Daniel was so convinced of this that he sought God's help to not only interpret a dream that King Nebuchadnezzar had, but to tell him what he had actually dreamed. Daniel had this to say regarding the telling and interpretation of the dream:

> *The king said to Daniel, whose name was Belteshazzar, Are you able to make known to me the dream which I have seen and the interpretation of it? Daniel answered the king, The (mysterious) secret which the king has demanded neither the wise men, enchanters, magicians, nor astrologers can show the king, but there is a God in heaven Who reveals secrets, and He has made known to King Nebuchadnezzar what it is that shall be in the latter days (at the end of days)* (Daniel 2:26-28).

We know that Daniel proceeded to tell the king the dream and then was divinely inspired to interpret what the Lord had revealed to him concerning the dream. Only someone who is acquainted with the Lord's ways can do such a thing.

Desire for God Alone

It would be easy to look at this and think how great Daniel was, but Daniel had developed this kind of relationship with God over the years. We must develop a desire for God alone, and not for what we can get out of God. Our heavenly Father knows everything about us, and He is quite qualified to give us what we need in this life to completely and totally satisfy us. The ones who know God believe Him and are able to do what they hear from God. They know within their hearts that they cannot do what they hear from God, unless He enables them to get this done. How does this kind of faith work? What motivates people to act on words that they believe are from God?

Jesus said that "The words I have spoken to you are spirit and they are life" (John 6:63). The words Jesus spoke then and continues to speak to us today are meant to enhance or prompt our spirits, giving us the ability to know that what we are hearing is coming from Him. The Scriptures say that as many as are led by the Spirit of God are called the children of God. If we are to be led, then we must hear the voice that is leading us. The words that Jesus speaks are meant to feed and satisfy our hunger for spiritual things. We are not only mind, will, and emotions, but our heavenly Father has also given us a spirit. Once our spirits became alive in Him through Christ, we have the ability to respond to His words in obedience.

> *For the (uttered) words that You gave Me I have given them/ and they have received and accepted (them) and have come to know positively and in reality (to believe with absolute assurance) that I came forth from Your presence, and they have believed and are convinced that You did send Me (John 17:8).*

We can be sure that God knows when we believe Him. Sometimes our belief is clouded with a bit of unbelief and doubt, but this is understandable in our early stages of knowing Christ. As we grow into maturity, we will still be challenged, as God's desire is to reveal more and more of Himself to us.

Now I have been sharing different testimonies about how

Being Intimate With God

God spoke to me and led me to do different things, not just
for myself, but for the benefit of others. As I was led along
by the Lord, I came to know Him better and to love Him
better. I began looking for opportunities to serve Him or for
Him to give me projects to do. I did this because I was
growing to love God more. I desired to hear Him speak because my heart was becoming more tender and sensitive to
Him. In the earlier stages of my coming to know Him more
intimately, I was afraid of what He might say to me—perhaps giving me things to do that I did not believe that I
could do—even sometimes feeling that He was angry with
me. But I soon learned that the more sensitive I became to
Him, the more capable I was of loving Him. And the more
capable of loving Him I became, the more open I was to listening to and obeying Him.

*So faith comes by hearing (what is told), and what
is heard comes by the preaching (of the message
that came from the lips) of Christ (the Messiah
Himself)* (Romans 10:17).

As we come to know Christ more fully, we also begin to
understand that what Christ does, He does because He loves
His heavenly Father. And as we grow to love God for ourselves, living by faith becomes a part of our lives. It becomes
natural to us to live by faith as we operate in relationship
and not out of duty. If we operate out of duty, then we do
not understand what it means to be personable with Christ.

*The Father dearly loves the Son and discloses to
(shows) Him everything that He Himself does* (John
5:20).

140

For (if we are) in Christ Jesus, neither circumcision nor uncircumcision counts for anything, but only faith activated and energized and expressed and working through love (Galatians 5:6).

Understanding Faith

As we grow familiar with Jesus Christ in prayer and in praising Him, He will reveal Himself to us. And as He does, we will come to better understand the things about faith that we have made complicated in our desire to please our heavenly Father. The grace of God will prevail, and we will understand how faith works. God speaks to us in His love for us—giving us responsibilities, talking with us in simple conversation, sharing His heart, showing us what is in our hearts, showing us our weaknesses and revealing to us His strength to overcome those weaknesses.

The way to understand faith better is to take Christ at His word. If we will do this, then we will be able to say as Jesus said: "The Father loves the Son." And because our heavenly Father loves us so much, we will then be able to execute His works with signs and wonders. These works will not be works that we do because we have to do them in order to feel better or to know that we are saved, but because we love Christ our Savior for all that He has done for us. Faith works because we love Christ so much that we are able, through our relationship with Him, to hear Him clearly and then follow instructions that are given to us by Him.

Now, we will understand more deeply that as we obey the Lord, our desire for Him increases because we begin to know first-hand that He loves and wants to be with us, showing us more about Himself.

Begin where you are. But do not be afraid to press forward. Cultivate a tender heart for Christ by responding to

Him where you are now. Do not try to use someone else's faith; although it is alright to use theirs as an example and to support us as we grow stronger in our own personal faith. Trust God, and He will teach you much about living by faith.

Chapter 22

The Surrendering Process

And anyone and everyone who has left houses or brothers or sisters or father or mother or children or lands for My name's sake will receive many (even a hundred) times more and will inherit eternal life (Matthew 19:29).

Do you not know that your body is the temple (the very sanctuary) of the Holy Spirit Who lives within you, Whom you have received (as a Gift) from God? You are not your own. You were bought with a price (purchased with a preciousness and paid for, made His own). So then, honor God and bring glory to Him in your body (1 Corinthians 6:19-20).

There is a saying that I often share with people, who sometimes want to take their lives into their own hands. I simply tell them: "You were bought with a price—the blood of Jesus Christ. You belong to Him. You were not put on a lay-a-way plan. Jesus has paid for you in full. Let Him determine what manner of life you should live."

A lay-a-way plan reminds me how some people will put

things on lay-a-way with full intentions of paying them off, but sometime lose the desire to have what they've put away, forgetting about the item and forfeiting their down payment. However, Jesus has not done this to us. He has paid for us in full.

It is hard to give up our lives to Christ, especially in the earlier stages of getting to know Him. Perhaps if we thought about it this way, the Lord has given His own blood for us, so He has legal rights to us. To read this, it may come across hard or harsh, but it is truth. If Christ paid for us with His own blood, then we are certainly dear to Him and He wants us around Him.

In my own walk with the Lord I continue to learn that yielding myself to Him really isn't difficult. I continue to learn that I am not giving up anything at all. It is more like an exchange—my life for His. Jesus is an excellent care-giver.

> *For whoever wants to save his (higher, spiritual, eternal) life, will lose it (the lower, natural, temporal life which is lived only on earth); and whoever gives up his life (which is lived only on earth) for My sake and the Gospel's will save it (his higher, spiritual life in the eternal kingdom of God)* (Mark 8:35).

> *I am the Good Shepherd. The Good Shepherd risks and lays down His (own) life for the sheep.....I am the Good Shepherd; and I know and recognize My own, and My own know and recognize Me...* (John 10:11,14).

Trusting God

Not very long ago I shared with someone who was having trouble letting go of themselves to Christ, that we need to simply yield. Primarily, we fear giving ourselves over to someone else because trust is a factor. We believe that if we have the strength and knowledge, we can do most anything; however, we cannot lead our own lives. I am not speaking of careers that we choose, but of learning to enjoy life from within our spirits, which have been brought alive to Christ, through His sacrifice.

Although living in Christ is meant to be a sacrificial lifestyle, sacrifices are not necessarily always difficult. It may seem so at the moment, but once we have seen the benefit of giving ourselves to Christ fully, we begin to approach sacrificing ourselves differently. I instructed my friend to yield his fear to the Lord. Admitting that we do not trust God in prayer will not surprise Him. We do not trust Him because we do not know Him.

One of the greatest struggles I had in moving away from home and pursuing God in other areas of my life was the fact that I did not trust Him.

"Don't hide the truth from Me," the Lord once told me emphatically. "Tell Me how you feel. If you do not trust Me, then tell Me." Now, thinking about such a comment from the Lord, one would think, *How can I not trust God?* Our minds will tell us that we can trust God—He is the Creator of all things. But we are not talking about trusting Him with everything else, but with ourselves. Quite honestly, if we can begin to trust God with ourselves—our lives, everything that concerns us—He will begin to show us how much He cares. Again, it takes faith to let go of ourselves. Faith is putting your trust in a Person—the Lord Jesus Christ. We belong to Him.

One of the simplest ways to learn to trust God is shared in two passages of Scripture.

In all your ways know, recognize, and acknowledge Him, and He will direct and make straight and plain your paths. Be not wise in your own eyes; reverently fear and worship the Lord and turn (entirely) away from evil (Proverbs 3:6-7).

Commit your way to the Lord (roll and repose each care of your load on Him); trust (lean on, rely on, and be confident) also in Him and He will bring it to pass. And He will make your uprightness and right standing with God go forth as the light, and your justice and right as (the shining sun of) the noonday (Psalm 37:5-6).

Now what does it mean to commit yourself to Christ? It means to commit your life—your ideas, what is important to you, what you put your hope and trust in—and surrender to Him those things that cause you to fight or become aggressive when you think about losing them. These things are important to Christ; He wants to be involved in your life.

It takes practice, but as we acknowledge Jesus, we will find that He is with us, living inside us. We will find that we do not have to fight and struggle so much. But we do have to give up our ideas about God. If they are true then He will allow us to hold onto them; however, if they are false, then God's truth will reveal them for what they are.

In this process of giving over ourselves to Christ, we will see how independent we really are. We want to remain the captain of our own ship, but as we gradually let go of ourselves to the Lord's control, we will find rest and peace.

Not long ago I was shopping online for a dresser for my room. The older one had become an eyesore, so I wanted something new. In my search I found the perfect piece of furniture—it was exactly what I wanted. However, the shipping cost for such a piece of furniture was substantial. The fact that the dresser was more expensive with the shipping costs did not dissuade me from wanting it. I believed in my heart that the Lord wanted me to purchase it. Now, I had already been looking in area stores to find the dresser, but could not. Finally, I went to the Lord in prayer and asked Him to lead me to where I could find the dresser so that I would not have to pay the shipping cost. He showed me two places. I went to one of those places and found the piece of furniture. The significance here is that I acknowledged Him and asked Him what to do before I purchased it online.

> *This was so that, by two unchangeable things (His promise and His oath) in which it is impossible for God ever to prove false or deceive us, we who have fled (to Him) for refuge might have mighty indwelling strength and strong encouragement to grasp and hold fast the hope appointed for us and set before (us)* (Hebrews 6:18).

Now if we are ever going to see that the Lord does not lie, we must allow Him regular deliberate influence into our lives. As we welcome Him, He will reveal His consistency and favor to us as His dearly loved children. We need to practice allowing the Lord freedom in our lives, which gives Him the freedom to show us who He is. It makes us more sensitive to Him as well as involves Him more quickly in our affairs. This kind of relating with our heavenly Father also makes us more aware of His Presence and desire to be involved with us regularly.

Chapter 23

Debts Paid

And He humbled you and allowed you to hunger and fed you with manna, which you did not know nor did your fathers know, that He might make you recognize and personally know that man does not live by bread only, but man lives by every word that proceeds out of the mouth of the Lord (Deuteronomy 8:3).

"Don't be afraid to trust Me," the Lord had been telling me. "I will take care of you. How will you know if I am Who I say that I am, if you do not trust Me?"

"Lord, I've never heard of such a thing. Now, you're telling me that you want me to go away for three months to a ministry training center and not pay my bills here for that amount of time? God, who will let me do that?"

This is a conversation that I had with the Lord some years ago. As I have shared in earlier chapters, the Lord has to get us to trust Him by getting us to give up what is important. In this particular incident, the Lord was requiring me to get training to be able to minister to people with special needs. However, being able to do this required my leaving my job for three months. My first thought was to fight with God; however, if we seek God for wisdom rather than fight Him, we will find that the things that we believe that we cannot do become doable in the light of God's wisdom.

"I am the Lord, and I will take care of you. This is what will happen. Go to those whom you owe money and let them know that you are going out of town for three moths to a training center for counselors. Tell them that you will begin paying your bills when you return. Do not tell them that I have told you this, as they will not understand. As surely as I live, I will take care of your debt. You are doing this at my command, and I will be with you."

"Oh...." It seemed pointless to argue.

I wasn't altogether arguing because I did not believe God, but because I had never done anything like this before. How could He make it work? After awhile, the Lord left me alone about it altogether, as far as reasoning with me concerning what to do. I knew that I had to make a quick decision about contacting my creditors. Although I did not have many of them, I still owed them money. It was almost time for me to leave for the training center, and I needed to do something as soon as possible. Since I wasn't able to pay three months of what I owed ahead of time, I had to do what the Lord was telling me to do.

"Larry," the Lord said to me, "the people to whom you owe money know you very well. You've always paid your bills, and they will trust you to do this. I know that it seems strange to you, but you have My favor already. Go now, and do what I am telling you to do."

Once I finally obeyed the Lord and requested of my creditors to allow me to pay my bills in full when I returned, they agreed. After I visited with them, I had peace. It was a long three months of intense training in the counseling center, but when I was finished I felt prepared to do what God was requiring of me to do. I was thinking that once the three months were over, God would come through miraculously and take care of all the bills I had, but that wasn't the case. Once the three months were over and I was stationed in a ministry position of counseling, it was still some time before God moved on His word. I was being challenged in every way, and it seemed as if God was not going to keep His word!

"How could You?" I asked. I was very upset with the Lord as I felt He had not kept His word to me. Time was passing, and I did not have the money to pay off my bills. "You always do this to me," I said, frustrated.

Many people give up when God does not do what they expect Him to do. If we are going to learn the way God does things, however, we must participate with Him from beginning to ending in the assignments that He gives us. Frustration is simply what we go through in learning to trust God to do things His way.

There were even times when I shook my fist toward heaven. Even so, I felt that God would come through somehow. Whenever He spoke to me in any situation, it always gave me hope that wasn't there before. For some reason, He was being quiet—not saying one word. I sensed that He was there with me, like a silent partner, but my restlessness was getting the best of me.

"I will help you through those whom you serve," He told me. "The workman is worthy of his hire, Larry, and I will repay you for what you are doing in My service. I am leading you to trust Me fully."

"Will I ever learn how to trust You?" I asked.

"You will, but you cannot do it in your own strength. Just believe Me. No man can live by natural food alone, but he lives by the rhema word that I speak to him. My word is written as it is, but it does not have the power to impact or change lives until it is spoken by the Spirit (My Spirit) which inspired the Scriptures in the beginning. It then has the power to bring to pass that which is spoken. I have told you that you will succeed, and that I will take care of you. This is what is going to happen."

"Thank You, Lord." I needed to hear that. I held on with everything that was within me, knowing that God would come through somehow and get me out of this financial situation.

"Lord," I said. "I am going to believe You, even if it destroys me. I'm going to trust You. If You fail, I fail. Remember Your promises to me, Lord. It is because of Your promises that I am kept alive and sustained in my hope toward You. Don't let me down, Father."

"I will not fail you."

I had been working with an individual who was in need of severe counseling assistance. He had been one of the worst recovering addicts I had ever met. Even the training center had not completely prepared me for this young man. After a long, tedious time of being with him and working with him—sitting up with him late at night, watching him go through DTs, listening to him cry for alcohol, and praying for him—he began to recover. Somehow, he realized that I wasn't going to leave him alone. He really needed my help at that time, and I needed God's help with him. I had forgotten about my own needs and began focusing on his. God showed me why I needed to help this young man, and that it would benefit him greatly. It did. He began to get better, so much better that he became a caring human being again. The drugs that he had abused changed him completely. It is amazing what severe drug addiction can do to the mind, will, and the emotions of a human being. It turns them into some kind of uncaring, sub-human being, with only a desire to save and look out for themselves. Bit by bit, I watched as he got better. One day, he talked to me about some things that really surprised me.

"I want to help you," he said. In spite of the fact that he had been severely addicted to drugs and alcohol, he was still very compassionate underneath, but desperately afraid to make friends and to open his heart to anyone. I had proven to him that I cared more about him than anything he could possibly offer. As he thought about how badly he had treated others who had tried to help him, he remembered how he had rejected them. I, on the other hand, had remained with him throughout the cleansing process and now the healing process of his mind.

"Oh?" I answered, not knowing what he meant by saying that he wanted to help me.

"Yeah. I have some money that was given to me. I want to help you," he said. "I will buy a van for the ministry, and I want to pay your personal bills for you. All of them."

He looked at me through hurting eyes with a sincerity that I seldom saw. He had been completely honest in everything he had communicated to me before—good or bad—and he was being serious now. He had seen my care and concern for him and knew that the ministry he had received was from the Lord. Because of his family background, he knew about the Lord, but he had never experienced Him as deeply as these past few difficult weeks.

The young man paid all the bills in one day. Nothing remained due. In addition to paying my bills, he purchased the van for the ministry as he had promised. God had loved him through some very difficult times. In fact, it was the most difficult time of his life. He had returned from the dead, literally, and could feel again.

Bless, (affectionately, gratefully praise) the Lord, O my soul, and forget not (one of) all His benefits (Psalm 103:2).

Chapter 24

He Will Instruct

Behold, He who keeps Israel will neither slumber nor sleep. The Lord is your keeper; the Lord is your shade on your right hand (the side not carrying a shield). The Lord will keep you from all evil; He will keep your life. The Lord will keep your going out and your coming in from this time forth and forevermore (Psalm 121:4-5, 7-8).

Some time back I shared with you what happened to my dad. The Lord was gracious to bring me home so that I could be there with him in his final days. It was a treasure to spend those days with him. Perhaps the best thing was how much the Lord cared about my feelings and how my dad's death could have hurt me, had I not known. I do not want to make it seem as if the Lord shows favoritism. I believe that His desire is to speak to each of us, giving us insight into the things that can hurt or harm us and even cause us deep sorrow. But even if He did not, our faith should be as such that God takes care of everything, and He does.

It wasn't long after my dad and mom passed away—both

in the same year—Dad in March and Mom in May, the Lord required me to leave home again. I could feel in my heart that it was time to leave my home, my birthplace, and everything that had been familiar to me again. There was nothing left for me to remain there. I felt finality within my heart. But the saddest thing was giving up my home. It is during times like this, when we feel the struggle to let go that we need to listen to the Lord the most. The Lord genuinely knows what it feels like to leave home—those things that are familiar, the things in which we have found our security. And since the earth belongs to Him and everything in it, the Lord is able to give us back what we believe we are giving up. The important thing is not what we are giving up, but what we are getting in return.

We have been speaking about being intimate with God. Part of being intimate with God—knowing His heart in matters—is being able to give up what we hold dear. When the Lord asks us to give something up, He has plans to give us something else that satisfies us more deeply than what we are actually giving up. But this is a process. If we are to get the full advantage of obeying the Lord's word to us, then we must obey with the right attitude. God does not mind our asking questions. He wants to give us wisdom, but above even this, He wants us to obey.

As I began to obey the Lord's heart to leave my home, land, and remaining family, things began to fall into place. I had much security in my hometown because it was familiar and I was well known and liked. Everything that I needed, the Lord had given me there. Quite honestly, if we can say that God has blessed us, then we should also be able to accept the idea that if God requires us to return what He has given us, then He is also able to replace it. This would not be the first time the Lord would require me to move, but each time I obeyed Him, I better understood how to communicate with Him. I believe I should elaborate here.

Obedience to the Lord should never be a dogmatic, rigid thing. We should desire to obey the Lord because we love Him. As we begin to obey Him, we will do it because we will see His answers, which will surprise and bless us. They will renew the strength we lose emotionally in between when He speaks and answers. This process has the tendency to tenderize us to the ways of the Lord. We experience God's word spoken to us and then see Him carry it out. We learn that God is sovereign, able to do things independently of us; however, as Father engages with us to carry out His will, we become partakers with Him in establishing His divine will. I believe that this cooperation with God enhances and feeds the emotional part of us that needs to see God working with us. It brings us security. God will more than likely speak something to us so that we can cooperate with Him by faith. This pleases God as we obey Him. It satisfies us as we see ourselves participating with Him in His righteousness and exercising the righteousness He has given us through Christ in every day life.

When I left home, I went to work with a faith ministry. Everything that came into the ministry came by the operation of faith. I had been taken from my home and put into a situation that I did not like in the least. The director of the ministry gave me a project right away that entailed cleaning and restoring an old house, a house that I was supposed to live in as it was being restored. When I arrived, I saw that it was run-down—the roof was almost gone and the yard was filled with weeds, tall grass, and thorn bushes that stuck to the flesh. The house had no furniture with the exception of an old kitchen table and a few chairs.

I worked diligently at getting all the thorn bushes out by

the roadside for pickup, and I made the house my sleeping quarters at night. For a while I felt joyful. I didn't know why, considering the situation. I just felt joyful and did the work with joy. Since I was very limited in what I could do because of the lack of tools, I had to stop and begin thinking about the situation. It would be getting cold soon, as fall and winter were approaching, and I only had a very old electric heater for warmth. The shower was cold. Very cold. There was no electric water heater in the house, and had there been, it could have very well been a fire hazard.

I remember one day I sat down and cried. Literally. I cried, all joy gone; I felt helpless. I felt as if the Lord had put me in a situation where I could do absolutely nothing. Even though I felt that I was in a terrible situation, I knew that God was able to do something, but when would He? How would He do it? Very few people knew me in this place, but the ministry was well known and liked. The director was well known for his many ministry exploits. He was very bold, courageous, and lived by faith. He had a family and depended on God to take care of them. I knew how to live by faith, but the problem for me had been, God wouldn't let me live by faith in one place. I was sure that He had sent me here to cause me to continue living by faith.

I was sitting in the front room of this old house one day, feeling as if the Lord had tricked me. Jeremiah felt the same way at one time. I felt as if God was playing a game with me, and that I was somehow trapped in the middle.

"What is wrong?" He asked.

"You know what is wrong," I said to Him. "I am angry, upset, and...oh, You know!" I was angry with Him, but I didn't want to tell Him.

"You need to tell Me how you feel. Just tell Me how you feel. You are angry with Me, aren't you?"

"Yes!" I said, sensing relief. "I am angry with You. You brought me here to this old, run-down house, and I can't do anything about it. How could You have done this?"

I pouted. I could not adequately express how angry I was toward the Lord.

"Just tell Me the truth. Let me know how you are feeling and that way we can talk about it. Tell Me, what do you see around you?"

"See?" I asked, still perturbed with my condition and trying to dry my teary eyes. "Lord, I see an old, run-down house. That's what I see. Really." In the same instance, however, I caught a glimpse of the house completely furnished. Somehow in my imagination, I saw this. But how could this be?

"Is that what you see?" He asked, and then I got a breath of fresh air. It seemed as if the Lord was trying to show me what could be, if I believed Him.

"That's what I see now, Lord," I responded, "but I know that you are able to fill this house with good things."

"Well said," the Lord told me. "Because you have seen what I see, I will give you the ability to fill this house with furniture that you like, colors that you like, and everything that makes it a home. I will never take anything away from you without paying it back. I will give back to you that which you have given Me. Likewise, whatever I give you, I will expect you to do well with it. If you are faithful in smaller things, then you can be trusted in bigger things. Just move back and I will show you that I am the Lord. Trust Me now, and do not be afraid. I have brought you here just to show you that I am the Lord and that I will not fail you in any way. I will draw you closer to Myself and cause you to trust Me more than you already do trust Me. You must grow and trust Me without failure, as I am with you, and I will cause My glory to shine about you. I will not in any way fail you. I am the Lord, and it is impossible for Me to lie to or deceive you. I will do things to confound you in your wisdom or what you believe you know and already know. This is only to show you that you cannot depend on your own wisdom or thinking, as it will fail and deceive you. I will not fail, nor will I deceive you. I have promised that I will be with you, and I will be. I am going to turn this house into a home for you, but do not plan on staying here. Plan to follow Me, as this is your lot in life, to know and follow after Me. I am training you to know Me intimately so that you can do all that I have called you to do without fail."

Shortly after the Lord had spoken these words to me, things began to drastically change. People from all around the area came to help refurbish this old house. Ultimately, it would be used as a halfway house for those recovering from addictions. And the Lord did everything He said. Not one word He spoke to me about restoring this house failed.

Nevertheless, My loving-kindness will I not break off from him, nor allow My faithfulness to fail (to lie and be false to him). My covenant will I not break or profane, nor alter the thing that is gone out of My lips (Psalm 89:33-34).

Chapter 25

With Me

Father, I desire that they also whom You have en-
trusted to Me (as Your gift to Me) may be with Me
where I am, so that they may see My glory, which
You have given Me (Your love gift to Me); for You
loved Me before the foundation of the world.....I
have made Your Name known to them and revealed
Your character and Your very Self, and I will con-
tinue to make (You) known, that the love which You
have bestowed upon Me may be in them (felt in
their hearts) and that I (Myself) may be in them
(John 17:24,26).

It has been many years since the Lord spoke to me concerning the promise that He and my mother made.

"Lord," my mother had said. "If you will give me a son, I
will return him to your service." Although we read this similar story in the book of Samuel, it is still hard for us to believe that God can still do the same thing today. God is
consistently and constantly concerned about having a relationship with us, and it does not have to be under special
circumstances, like some would feel that He and my mother

had. Having spent so much time with my heavenly Father, I realize that He loves all of us so very much.

One of the hardest processes that any of us will go through in getting to know God is the transforming process of our minds. Because of the lies of Satan we believe the worse about ourselves—yet we believe that we can accomplish many things on our own if God will help or assist us. We must believe with all sincerity that God is our life. He is the lifegiver. It has taken me many years to believe and accept this. Even now the Lord is teaching me that our lives are not composed of one successive blessing after the other, but learning to accept His Word, not so much the written scriptures as we have them in written form, but the spoken Word of God that is instant and able to lead us in any direction, regardless of whether it is for ministry or not. Our lives should not be limited to one ministry function after the other. There will always be those who need ministry, but we are not created to be ministers. We are created to give away the glory of God as it is revealed to us as it was lived and revealed through Jesus Christ. Simply put this means that what God reveals to us about Himself, we are then to pass it on to the rest of His Body. If we do this, God is able to have a flowing of His presence from one life to the other, as we all grow to know Him together. This is not always done in large churches where you have someone preaching the Gospel, but in any setting where there can be conversation about the Lord.

I have given to them the glory and honor which You have given Me, that they may be one (even) as We are one: I in them and You in Me, in order that they may become one and perfectly united, that the world may know and (definitely) recognize that You sent Me and that You have loved them (even) as You have loved Me (John 17:22- 23).

My sincerest desire and I believe also that it is the Lord's desire that we do not take the things that I have written in this book as things that were revealed to a special person—perhaps someone who struggled to know God. That is not the intent. I realize that there are wonderful testimonies. I realize that they may seem unreachable. However, we must understand that I did nothing to accomplish anything, except believe and have faith in Christ Jesus. He did everything else, and I am sure He will continue to assist all of us as well. Remember when John said this:

> *We are writing about the Word of Life (in) Him Who existed from the beginning, Whom we have heard, Whom we have seen with our (own) eyes, Whom we have gazed upon (for ourselves) and have touched with our (own) hands.....What we have seen and (ourselves) heard, we are also telling you, so that you too may realize and enjoy fellowship as partners and partakers with us. And (this) fellowship that we have (which is a distinguishing mark of Christians) is with the Father and with His Son Jesus Christ (the Messiah). And we are now writing these things to you so that our joy (in seeing you included) may be full (and your joy may be complete)* (1 John 1:1,3-4).

Recently, I have taught messages about learning to intermingle with Christ. All you need do is begin acknowledging Him every day. It may seem repetitious in the early stages to keep saying, "Lord, I acknowledge you. Lead me."

However, as those who were taught by Jesus began to do this, the Lord began to speak to them, giving them insight in varying areas about how to get things done or buy things that they needed. He led them because they acknowledged Him. After we do this for a while, it gets to the place where our hearts automatically ask or consider Christ, and He leads us accordingly. As we see this apparent presence of His at work in our lives, we will begin to hunger for more. This kind of apparent and constant presence of God gives us hope, strengthens our faith, and enables us to see what we cannot see through hope alone. Christ is living with us. He is within us.

As I close out this book I am reminded of how I walked away from my home all those years ago—hurting and crying as I went—uncertain of what would happen in the new city where the Lord was sending me; however, God prevailed. All these years later I began to have dreams about a home—my home. In a dream, which I had twice, I saw myself sitting in a yard. All that I owned—furniture, dog, etc., were there with me. The furniture was covered. It was as if I were waiting to be able to move into a home. Although the Lord never said one word to me in this dream, I knew that it meant I would have a place to live, and now I do.

Last year the Lord began to speak to me about looking for my own home. Since I'd just started a church fellowship, I said to Him, "Lord, I would rather not at this time," thinking it could harm or put pressure on the church financially. However, the pressure from His Spirit rested upon me. Eventually, we recognize the Spirit of God. Much like we have weight, so does the Lord, and just as our own personal body weight can pressure people, so can the weight of our heavenly Father. His weight was leading me to buy my own home.

I honored what I felt by shopping for homes online. I had never before looked for a home. But God led me in this. I had yet another dream. I had mentioned to the Lord the kind of house that I would like, and in the dream, the house came alive. I loved the house that I saw in this vision. The dream was quick—only seconds, and then I awoke.

Not long after this—days as a matter of fact—I was searching again for homes online. I ran across this one house that was beautiful. It was too beautiful. I felt in my heart that I could never afford such a home because it was simply too nice. But over the next few days, the Lord continued to press it upon my heart to go back to this house that I had seen, and it was one of the only ones that I had sincerely loved.

"But I cannot afford that house," I told the Lord.

"One of the reasons why you have not been satisfied with the homes you've looked at is because you are pricing them too cheaply," He said. "Look for a home that you have prequalified for, and you will be happy." So I did what He told me to do.

Consequently, the house that I did not think I could afford fell into that price range. I went to look at other houses before I went to this one, but something just did not click on the inside. Finally, I went to the one I had liked so much. I can remember the excitement I felt when I went to the house. Before I ever saw it on the inside, I felt an inner charge, telling me that this was the house. When I saw it setting there on the corner, I knew that it was mine.

It was funny, but when I went inside the house, standing just inside the door, I thought to myself: *I have been here before.* Then the Lord reminded me that it was the house I had seen in the dream. Everything about this house fit the dream. I knew that I was home.

I had lived in one place for eight years. It was hard for me to believe that I could get a house that fit me so well. It was exactly what I had hoped for, although I would have never been able to describe the way it felt to be in a home where things fit. But I will say that the house was filled with the same feeling I have had in walking with the Lord and obeying Him. It was one of peace, safety, and serenity. A holy quiet seemed to calm everything—including my soul. I had perfect peace.

"Can it be?" I asked the Lord.

"Many years ago, you gave Me your home," the Lord told me. "I am simply giving you a home in return. You have given Me your life, so I am giving you My life in return. I will never ask you to give Me anything, that I am not willing to give in return. You sowed your natural life, so I am sowing My spiritual life back to you. All these years I have been enabling you to get your credit established, so that you would be able to have a place of rest—a home on the earth."

I cannot tell us how wonderful being in my own home feels. I am at perfect rest and peace, and God continues to speak with me intimately. It is not in the abundance of things, gifts, or blessings, but it is in Christ that life sincerely pours forth. Out of every blessing and experience that Christ has afforded me, none compares to His intimate, social presence.

As we consider walking with Him, the Lord will help us to know Him. He will show Himself in a special, significant way, so that we will recognize Him. As we hunger for Him, He will show Himself. Never allow the devil to tell you that you are wasting your time serving God. If you listen to him, he will rob you of the joy of knowing Christ intimately. However, if you pursue Him by the simple teachings shared in this book, the Lord will reveal Himself to you and walk with you on an intimate basis. He will show Himself. It may not be easy in the early stages—expect conflict from within and without. The Lord will keep you as you seek to know Him intimately.

> *And anyone and everyone who has left houses or brothers or sisters or father or mother or children or lands for My name's sake will receive many (even a hundred) times more and will inherit eternal life* (Matthew 19:29).

About the Author

Larry B. Reese is founder and president of RAFFA Front-Line Ministries and RAFFA Discipleship School. His ministry is recognized for its practicality and simplicity. As an ordained prophet, Larry has an intense desire and passion to train God's people to know, recognize, and better understand their heavenly Father. With many years of personal experience with God, Larry imparts the wisdom and techniques the Father has afforded him into the lives of the students enrolled in the Raffa Discipleship School. He teaches God's children how to be intimate with Him. Mr. Reese is available for conferences and seminars for spiritual growth and development.

To contact the author:
Web address: www.raffafrontline.org